General Editor: NATHANIEL TARN

The Human Sciences & Philosophy

Lucien Goldmann

Translated by Hayden V. White
and Robert Anchor

JONATHAN CAPE
THIRTY BEDFORD SQUARE
LONDON

Available in the United States from
Grossman Publishers, Inc.

First published in Great Britain 1969
Reprinted 1970
By Jonathan Cape Ltd, 30 Bedford Square, London WC1
Translated from the French *Sciences Humaines et Philosophie*
© 1966 by Société Nouvelle des Editions Gonthier, Paris
English translation © 1969 by Jonathan Cape Ltd

CAPE Paperback edition ISBN 0 224 61547 5
    Hardback edition ISBN 0 224 61548 3
GROSSMAN Paperback edition 670–38644–8
        Hardback edition 670–38643–x

Printed in Great Britain by Richard Clay (The Chaucer Press),
Ltd, Bungay, Suffolk

Contents

GENERAL EDITOR'S NOTE

Dr Lucien Goldmann's *Sciences Humaines et Philosophie* was first published in 1952 by the Presses Universitaires de France; the text from which this English version was taken appeared in the Collection *Médiations*, Éditions Gonthier (Paris, 1966). It contains a new Preface which appears in our volume.

With Dr Goldmann's permission I have added a few items to his footnotes where I felt that the general reader, as well as a number of specialists unacquainted with the French sociological scene in the nineteen fifties, would be likely to benefit. These notes are as systematic as possible, though they've had to be selective and, in a few cases, the complexities of multi-national bibliography and the paucity of references have been too great for me. In any event, the added notes are marked *Ed. Note* to distinguish them from Dr Goldmann's originals.

PREFACE TO THE NEW EDITION

To the memory of Lucien Sebag

This book has two aspects. Originally they were intimately connected, but at this time it will be well to distinguish between them. The first, or theoretical, side offers no special problems, for it represents in general the position I still hold on the matter.[1] But the second, or polemical, side may have only an historical interest in as much as it consists of a criticism of thinkers who dominated Western sociology around the year 1952. During the last fourteen years sociology has undergone a fundamental change, and today it is dominated by other currents and different personalities. And while one might think that a polemicist would rejoice in the fact that his opponents had lost part or all of their influence, actually this is not the case at all, which renders the polemical problem all the more important.

Philosophical discussions never take place in a vacuum, and it may happen, as in the present case, that the disappearance of one of the parties in a debate will result in its replacement, not by currents favoured by the other, but by ideologies that are completely different and whose nature is as negative and as questionable as those which the first party had originally opposed. This is what has in fact happened in French sociological thought, which is our special concern.

The debate between Georges Gurvitch and myself took place against the background of a shared set of humanistic values and a common belief in the historical nature of the whole of social reality.

Viewing the matter in a somewhat larger perspective, it could be said that these two elements constituted the main bases of philosophical discussion between 1910 and a time which, at least in France, falls somewhere between 1955 and 1960. The principal participants in these discussions were above all the Existentialist philosophies, which tended – with Heidegger and Sartre – towards the construction of philosophies of history, Christian thought, and Hegelian and Marxist thinking. Georges Gurvitch, an independent and original thinker, operated well within the confines of these discussions, despite his relativism.

Future historians of Western society and culture will probably see the period 1955–60 in France as a turning point, on the sociological plane, from 'crisis capitalism' to 'organized capitalism' (*capitalisme d' organisation*), and, correspondingly, on the level of thought, from a philosophical – historical and humanistic – sociology to the ahistorical sociology of the present time. To be sure, this change did not take place overnight; like all such changes, it occurred slowly, over a long period of time. The important problem is to determine its nature and the epoch in which the qualitative transformation occurred.

The term 'crisis capitalism' indicates the period in which the free market was disrupted by the formation of trusts and monopolies and European society was shaken by a series of social and political crises, one following closely upon another, each of which it successfully met (though only with great difficulty), resulting in the creation of an equilibrium that turned out to be only temporary and that was soon dissolved (by the First World War, the revolutionary movements of 1917–23, the economic crises of 1929–33, Nazism, the Second World War, and the development, on the confines of European industrial society, of Italian Fascism and the Spanish Civil War). By the term 'organized capitalism', we mean the contemporary period which, through the creation of regulative mechanisms owing to state interventions, has made possible a continual economic growth and the diminution, not to say the total elimination, of internally generated social and political crises.[2] The intellectual movement corresponding to organized capitalism is to be found in the replacement of a philosophical tradition concerned with the problems of anxiety and death (or, conversely, with historical and transcendental hope) by a scientistic, rationalistic and ahistorical mode of thinking. This new rationalism differs radically from that of the Enlightenment, which served as the philosophical world view of the rising middle class, by virtue of its abandonment of the humanistic and individualistic values informing the latter.

Leaving aside the considerable growth of a positivistic, empiricist technique of investigation (which is purely descriptive and is, for that very reason, debateable on the theoretical level), this change is marked by one particularly striking fact: in Western European intellectual life, and especially in France, two social sciences have taken over the ideological role formerly played by philosophy. These social sciences are sociology and anthropology.

The thinkers who today play the role formerly filled by Bergson, Meyerson, Bruschvig, Sartre, Jean Wahl or Merleau-Ponty arc, above all, Claude Lévi-Strauss, an anthropologist, and Raymond Aron, a sociologist who began his intellectual career as a philosopher of history during the preceding period. Aron still honours many of the values associated with liberal capitalism, even though today he simultaneously defends the opposed values of organized capitalism and its peculiar form of liberalism. Thus, in the evolution of contemporary sociology, Aron especially seems to represent a transitional phase between two essentially different eras.

By contrast, Lévi-Strauss, an exceptionally sophisticated theorist whose links with contemporary society are certainly unconscious and involuntary and are mediatized in complex ways, represents current tendencies in thought in a different manner: he is the exponent of a formalistic system that tends to eliminate in a radical way all interest in history and the problem of meaning.[3]

The truly decisive fact in the evolution of contemporary French sociology is to be found in the emergence of a rather large number of sociologists, roughly forty or fifty years of age. These already occupy important places in the ever tighter organization of the sociological research which, over the last fifteen years, has become increasingly dominated by the Centre d'Études Sociologiques on the one hand and by independent, or interrelated, institutes or centres on the other. The web of interrelations, positions and university influence of these sociologists constitutes an ever more rigid organization which defines the main lines of current investigation. Although they command an ideological influence much weaker than that enjoyed by philosophical thinkers of the preceding generation, they possess none the less an incomparably greater administrative power over the orientation of research.

All this has resulted in a mass of works which are more numerous, larger and better developed on the quantitative level, but which are also, for the most part, more routine in nature and all but destitute of significant theoretical elaboration.

A study of contemporary sociology that would identify the various currents of these works would show, we think, the extent to which they share a common ahumanistic, ahistorical and aphilosophical attitude; which is to say that all of them favour, implicitly or explicitly, the current technocratic society.

We are not given to dividing intellectual work according to age and generation, but it should be noted in this provisional account that, for a while, there was some evidence that the younger generation of sociologists were beginning to develop their theoretical capacities in a most striking manner. With the death of Lucien Sebag, French social science unhappily lost a young thinker of truly outstanding talent, one who justified great hopes for the future Other recent works produced by this generation also gave, at first glance, the impression that a truly *critical* sociology was in process of formation. Actually, however, on closer inspection, it can be seen that, up to the present at least, this critical capacity has been brought to bear solely on the vestiges of traditional liberal society and on the problem of the human costs of change, and almost never on the modern society in process of being born, a society that is dangerous for intellectual and cultural life in another way. The emerging society, dominated especially by mass production and consumption, runs the risk (as we noted on another occasion) of creating as its principal mass product a host of 'illiterate scholars'.

These observations suggest the urgent need of composing a work similar to mine but dealing with the sociologists of the current generation. For the moment, however, we must remain content with a mere mention of the most important of the intellectual and methodological principles which seem to us to confirm the ahistorical nature of the greater part of current sociological reflection: the disjunction of the ideas of structure and function. If structures in fact characterize the reactions of men to different problems which their relations with the surrounding social and natural world raise, these structures always fulfil, in a particular context, *a function* within a larger social structure. And when the situation changes, they cease to fulfil this function and thus lose their rational character, which leads men to abandon them and to replace them with new and different structures. It is thus that the indissoluble link between structure and function, resulting from the relatively durable nature of functions and the relatively provisional nature of structures, constitutes the motive power of history or, to put it another way, the historical character of human behaviour. Thus, if one separates structure from function, he has already committed himself to the creation of *either* an ahistorical and formalistic structuralism or a functionalism with the same orientation. The structuralism will be oriented towards the investigation of the most generalized structures of thought, which can be found in all social forms and which are never affected by historical changes, thereby eliminating by its very methodology the historical element from its field of study. The functionalism, which is interested only in the conservative nature of every institution and mode of behaviour within a given society, illuminates it by revealing its 'functional' aspect, but never confronts the problem of change. These are but two sides of one coin. The manner in which the functionalist designates what he calls 'dysfunctions' indicates how these have only a negative character for him; these dysfunctions are related only to the society under study, without considering whether what is designated as 'dysfunctional' might not perhaps be a new functionality in process of constitution in relation to a new social order or at least in relation to a new social situation. The very use of the term 'dysfunction' indicates the limits of this perspective, limits which are ultimately the same as those of non-genetic structuralism: *the methodological denial of any historical dimension to social facts.*

It should be noted that a few recent works have tried to recover the historical dimension and rightly stress the ahistorical nature of non-genetic structuralism and functionalism; but instead of really questioning them, they recognize rather their study of symbolic expressions and of social relations as valid, thereby identifying history with an abstract progression that has nothing to do with the real lives of men. These works appear to us to be, in the last analysis, completely ahistorical.

Thus, at a time when the most creative literary and artistic endeavours from the *nouveau roman* to the films of Godard, Robbe-Grillet, Visconti, Antonioni and Resnais, concentrate on the inhuman and anti-cultural character of organized capitalism, and on the difficulty of adjusting to it, contemporary sociology moves towards an alliance with this form of capitalism and even becomes, in a theoretical sense, a constitutive element in it, or its implicit defender. At this point, a humanist must criticize this sociology, and oppose it.

In conclusion, we would like to raise a final problem: whatever the dangers of this sociology, which is an important constitutive element in the emerging organized capitalism, any debate with it must be carried out above all on the question of its scientific value. Is it truly operative? Does it allow us to understand the phenomena which it studies and especially the contemporary Western society with which it is intimately connected? On this point, of course, the answer will not be easily found, but it ought not to be equivocal.

In fact, we have just said that the main theoretical currents of contemporary social science (as well as the positivistic and bitty research which grows constantly in scope and weight), which we have already criticized in the present work, loses sight of the qualitative changes in social structures and of the historical dimension of human facts. Now, as long as the fundamental human values that animated social group behaviour were subject to a continual and more or less rapid change, this dimension was *essential*, as much for the comprehension of the facts studied as for the comprehension of sociological thought itself, of which these values constitute a basic element.

But for some centuries now, we have had one value that is changeless and is shared by all social groups, *the control of nature*. This value has permitted the construction of an important corpus of physicochemical sciences that are at once ahistorical, nondialectical and extremely efficacious in an operational sense.

In the human sciences, however, all attempts to provide equivalents of the so-called 'exact' sciences have yielded very little in the way of positive results. The very least that we can say is that today we have arrived at a particularly important turning in the evolution of Western society, a turning marked by the appearance of self-regulating economic mechanisms. And if, as we have observed recently in an article on this problem, a society were to be constituted which, by means of similar self-regulating mechanisms, concentrated the direction of society in the hands of specialists in all domains and assured to the majority of men a more or less rapid but continual rise in their standard of living, while consigning them to the status of simple administrators who are more or less passive and devoid of genuine responsibilities, then the question arises as to whether this does not imply a role for the social sciences different from that which they have played in the past and which would permit them to function in much the same way as the physical sciences.

Actually, this idea of a radical rupture in the heart of the historical process, considered as a future prospect, was a preoccupation of the great dialectical thinkers of the late nineteenth and early twentieth centuries. Hegel's conception of the end of History and the moment of Absolute Self-Consciousness and the Marxist notion of the end of Prehistory and the beginning of History corresponded to the idea of a qualitative transformation as a result of which our knowledge of man and society would become objective and transparent.

In a less utopian, more pessimistic and sometimes even desperate way, some of the most important thinkers and writers of our own time have perceived a similar transformation. If we used structuralist terms to characterize it, this transformation would be marked by the crystallization of a social order endowed with regulative mechanisms sufficiently refined and developed to deprive both the technological power of transforming nature as well as inter-human relations (in so far as these enjoy a relative autonomy with respect to technology) of any capacity to effect significant change in the basic values governing human behaviour in society. This result could be obtained, on the one hand, by reducing the responsibilities individuals have in their work to a minimum and eliminating the compulsion hitherto provided by an inadequate standard of living and the scarcity of goods, so that the problem of values would no longer be raised to a level sufficiently intense to permit them to act effectively on an individual's behaviour. On the other hand, the values accepted by the dominant group would assure continued technical progress, without any reflexive effect on their own nature, and the techniques of economic and social intervention commanded by this group would permit it to correct social imbalances that might lead to the questioning of the dominant values by the 'administrators'.

In such a society, values (I am not very sure that it is still possible to speak of wisdom on the level of their most conscious acceptance) might attain to a status almost as durable as the pursuit of the technical domination of nature in the domain of the physical and natural sciences.

An ahistorical sociology could then acquire a real operative value, since an extremely important sector of the social life would be characterized by the persistence of fundamental norms for the regulation of conduct. No doubt this science would have less to do with the basis and essence of human reality than with appearances, but the problem of essence would have become less urgent in the extent to which its manifestations had been successfully rendered durable.

It must still be determined if this prospect – however strong the tendencies leading in its direction, however great the opportunities (or dangers) it offers – constitutes for thinkers committed to Western humanistic values a desirable, a tolerable or a distinctly dangerous possibility.

Whatever the individual thinker may conclude, it is necessary that he arrive at his assessment in full consciousness, which means, among other things, for the sociologist, that he must understand the main currents of contemporary sociology, the nature of their relation to contemporary social reality, the direction of their movement at the centre of this reality, and the social frameworks which are capable of promoting or, conversely, of reducing their positive value as instruments of knowledge.

Although we cannot develop the point at length in this brief preface, we should stress that our criticism of organized capitalism (or, to use another term for the same thing, of consumer society, the society of mass production) is not intended to lead back to the past or to question the positive achievements of modern society (its raising of the standard of living, its regulative mechanisms which allow society to avoid particularly severe crises, etc.), just as Marx's classic criticism of capitalism was not meant to suggest that one could or should seek to return to the society of the Middle Ages. But recognition of the genuine achievements of a social order provides no reason for closing one's eyes to its negative and dangerous aspects. Whether we like it or not, the evolution of industrial societies has created some irreversible situations, and the sociologist (like the whole of society) must determine whether he can accept the spontaneous tendencies of an evolutionary course oriented towards an increasingly technocratic structure, or if, conversely, there exists a chance of salvaging all the achievements that such a development is capable of contributing to the realization of an economic democracy. This prospect seems to us to imply, in the light of present experiences, the necessity of a self-regulation of industrial enterprises and of social institutions which would permit above all *a democratization of responsibilities*, the only means of meeting the considerable intellectual dangers created by current developments.

INTRODUCTION

To Émile Bréhier, with respect and gratitude

When we began this book, we thought of entitling
it *Introduction to Methodological Problems in the
Sociology of Knowledge*. During the writing of it,
however, we discovered that it turned upon the problem of the relations between the human sciences and
philosophy.

This was bound to happen. If philosophy is more
than a simple conceptual expression of different world-
views, if, apart from its *ideological* character, it also
reveals certain *fundamental truths concerning the
relations of men with other men and of men with
the universe*, then these truths must be found also at
the very basis of the human sciences and in their
methods in particular.

All philosophy is, among other things, philosophy of
consciousness and of the mind (without being thereby
necessarily Idealistic). The philosophies of nature,
from the Renaissance down to Schelling and Hegel,
tried to introduce mind and consciousness into the
physical world. The development of the physical
sciences seems to have proven that this attempt was
ill-conceived. The physical sciences developed at the
expense of nature-philosophy, which had to abandon
the field. From this historical experience one idea
emerged which was *valid for the physical world
until further notice: a realm of knowledge can right-
fully be claimed by positive science to the extent to
which it frees itself from interference by philosophy*.

Scientism tried to extend this approach to the biological and human sciences, recommending a mechanistic biology, behaviouristic psychology, an empiricist history, and a factual and descriptive sociology.

If scientism is right, philosophy itself is an ideological relic that no longer has any raison d'être and from which we must be liberated.*

But if, on the other hand, philosophy really tells us something about the nature of man, then every attempt to destroy it necessarily obstructs the understanding of human reality. In this case, the human sciences will have to be philosophical *in order to be scientific*.

The study of method in the human sciences *on the plane of positive science itself* poses the problem of the uselessness or, conversely, the present value of philosophy. This problem provides the background of our study.

Before ending this introduction, we should like to thank Professor Émile Bréhier who inspired us to reflect on problems of method and without whose help this study would probably never have been completed.

---

* We once heard a secretary at an Institute of Psychology explaining to a young student who had just enrolled that statistics were on the curriculum 'in order to prevent psychology from degenerating into philosophy'.

I

HISTORICAL THOUGHT AND ITS OBJECT

Every social fact is a historical fact and vice versa. It follows that history and sociology *study the same phenomena* and that each of them grasps some real aspect of these phenomena: but the image which each discipline gives of them will necessarily be partial and abstract in so far as it is not completed and qualified by the findings of the other. Now, the transition from the abstract to the concrete is not achieved by merely adding together two partial images. Knowledge of human reality is not attained by uniting the *partial* and *distorting* conclusions of a factual (*chosiste*) or psychologistic sociology with those of a political or simply positivistic history. Concrete knowledge is not a *sum* but a *synthesis* of *justified* abstractions. In the present case as the abstractions *are not justified*, their sythesis is impossible. It is not, then, a matter of combining the findings of sociology and history but of abandoning all abstract sociology and all abstract history in order to achieve a concrete science of human reality, which can only be a *historical sociology* or a *sociological history*. This is the thesis which we shall attempt to defend in this study.

Sociology cannot be *concrete* unless it is historical, just as history, if it wishes to go beyond the mere recording of facts, must necessarily become explicative, that is to say, more or less sociological.

History, historical sociology and philosophy of

history all pose a preliminary epistemological problem. Why is man interested in *certain facts, which are unique and localized in time?*[1] Why is man interested in the past, and above all what in the past interests him?

At first glance the answer seems simple: the object of history is to provide knowledge, as *rigorous* and *precise* as possible, of events in their *specificity* and *particularity*, without any regard for individual or collective interest or practical utility. The historian is a scholar who seeks the truth as an end in itself and not as a means to some other end; it is not necessary to ask why he seeks it: *Adequatio rei et intellectus* is the general aim of all scientific activity. As for the means to be used, they are also obvious: disinterested-ness, erudition, critical spirit, devotion to the task, not to mention native intelligence and acumen which can be taken for granted.

If one looks more closely, however, the problem proves to be somewhat more complex. Since modern physics had to establish itself in the sixteenth and seventeenth centuries by a bitter struggle against *theological* and *social* pressure of all kinds, it stressed above all the necessity of *disinterested* research. In doing so, it contributed to the creation of a scientistic ideology which regarded *all* research and *all* factual knowledge as valuable in themselves and viewed with a certain contempt any effort to link scientific thought to any practical use or to the satisfaction of human needs. One might say that modern society has re-deemed the faults of the past and made up for the sufferings of the pioneers of science by venerating and respecting all the more avidly anyone who continues or purports to continue their work. The extreme con-sequences of this scientistic ideology appear above all in the human sciences, where countless pure scholars pass their lives accumulating a maximum of knowledge in a small, limited and partial field and believe themselves to be anthropologists, historians, linguists, philosophers and so forth.

To be sure, this attitude, even in its side effects, had and still has its use and its justification. Scientific research requires freedom and independence from all external interference. Similarly, it demands of the researcher, not that he renounce all ideology, but that he make every possible effort to subordinate ideology to the reality of the facts he is studying in his work. Such are the requirements expressed in the demand for disinterested research.

As for the high value placed on erudition as such, that is also justified, on two counts: first, since erudition – being an indispensable prerequisite of all serious research – is inevitably, though indirectly, coming to be valued by society, so the esteem in which it is held, and the demand that writers should have a thorough knowledge of the subjects they write about, is clearly having a salutary effect on the level of scientific work. Secondly, pure erudition is justified by the fact that it is impossible to know in advance *either the scientific or the practical importance* of a complex of facts as yet inadequately explored. Undoubtedly, there are certain purely scholarly investigations which represent a waste of time and energy, but this waste is the unavoidable cost of exploratory work; and experience has shown that the support and absolute freedom of all research, without concern for any practical use which it might offer at the outset, is still the most profitable attitude *from the viewpoint of utility itself*.

None of this should obscure, however, a *fundamental epistemological truth*, put forward as early as 1846 by Marx in his *Theses on Feuerbach* and

25

stressed again more recently by Jean Piaget in his psychological and epistemological research. Human thought in general, and therefore scientific thought, which is a particular aspect of it, are closely related to human conduct and to the effects man has on the surrounding world. Although it may be *an end in itself for the researcher*, scientific thought is only a *means* for the social group and for humanity as a whole.

Now, from this point of view, the practical utility of the physico-chemical sciences is obvious. They constitute the foundation of all technology; they are the means, not only of prediction, as Auguste Comte would have it, but also of producing, dominating and transforming the world.[2] But this obvious fact itself raises the problem of the basis of the historical sciences. Of what use is the knowledge of unique events, which are irretrievably localized in time and space, especially when one is dealing with past events?

Let us immediately rule out the idea that the principal purpose of history is to provide lessons which teach men how to act in the present or in the future *in order to realize the goals* which they set for themselves. It is obvious that conditions change radically and that one does not learn from the history of the Punic Wars, for example, how to win a battle today, nor from the history of the French or English revolutions how to resolve problems posed by revolutions in our own time. From this point of view, the pragmatic value of the historical sciences is almost nil, and we might well view them as the typical case of a purely erudite and disinterested science.

It seems to us, however, that this would be to confuse the *necessarily disinterested* character of the individual scientific investigation with the quite different character of every system of knowledge which, envisaged in its social function, is *necessarily bound to practice and to life*. When men and social groups study history, they are only secondarily looking for means, that is to say processes and techniques; they are looking primarily for *values and ends*.

The problem of the *ontological* and *epistemological* foundations of history is a particular aspect of the general ontological problem of the relations of man to his kind, which certain contemporary philosophers, taking their point of departure from Descartes, have called the problem of the 'Other', but which could be called more precisely the problem of the 'We'. This is not a simple play on words, but one of the most important points of departure in modern philosophy.

'*Ego sum, ego existo*,' wrote Descartes, thus stressing that *ego* which has remained the foundation of all rationalist and empiricist philosophy ever since, from the monads of Leibniz, the sensationalism of the empiricists, the *ego* of Fichte, and even the radically separated attributes of Spinoza, up to our own time, where, in our high-school grammars we are taught as a self-evident truth that: 'The *je* has no plural. *Nous* is *je* and *tu*.'[3] From this point of view, the *ego* is regarded as the primary fundamental datum, the point of departure; and the problem of the relations between men, when it is raised, necessarily becomes the problem of the 'Others'. 'Other' men are assimilated to the physical and sensible world. They are no more than things that I observe and understand just as I observe and understand a falling stone. It is not surprising then, to discover that if there is indeed a rationalist or empiricist history, there cannot be from either standpoint, a *philosophy of history*. Because, for the rationalist and empiricist, the past is past in *a radical and simple* way, having no existential importance, either for the present or the future.

As against that, dialectical thought begins with a somewhat extreme statement, almost a manifesto proclaiming the radical change that was just being effected in philosophical thought. To the *ego* of Montaigne and Descartes, Pascal responds, 'The I is odious,' and from Hegel to Marx, 'other' men become more and more, not beings which I see and understand, but beings *with whom I act in common*. They are no longer *on the object side* but *on the subject side* of knowledge and action. The 'We' thus becomes the fundamental reality with respect to which the 'I' is subsequent and derivative. In our own time, one of the greatest revolutionary poets, Bertold Brecht, formulated this position in terms which, unintentionally, repeat the sentence of Bruneau while reversing the accent. To the colonial capitalist who asks a coolie to sacrifice himself for his business, which he presents to him as a common civilizing effort, the coolie responds, 'We and I and You are not the same thing.' The meaning is obvious: there is only a 'We' where there is a genuine community. Now, in the so-called common enterprise, the worker seeks his wages, the capitalist his profit. The transition from the false situation of 'I and You' to the conscious and authentic 'We' is the very question upon which historical epistemology is founded.

It is from this standpoint that we must view the problem with which we began. The ontological basis of history is the relation of men with other men, the fact that the individual 'I' exists only against the background of the community. We are seeking in knowledge of the past *the same thing that we are seeking in knowledge of contemporary men*, above all the fundamental attitudes of individuals and of human groups with respect to values, *the community and the universe*. If knowledge of history has any practical importance for us, it is because we learn from it, about men who, in *different* circumstances and with *different* means, for the most part inapplicable in our own time, fought for values and ideals which were similar, identical, or opposed to those of today; and this makes us conscious of belonging to a totality which transcends us, which we support in the present and which men who come after us will continue to support in the future. The historical consciousness exists only for an attitude which has gone beyond the individualistic 'I', and it is precisely one of the principal means of this going beyond. For rationalism the past is only an error, knowledge of which is useful for throwing light on the progress of reason; for empiricism it is a mass of real facts which, as such, are fixed in relation to a conjectural future. Only the dialectical attitude can achieve a synthesis by understanding the past as a *necessary and valid stage and path towards the common action of men of the same class in the present in order to realize an authentic and universal community in the future.*

What men seek in history are the transformations of the acting subject in the dialectical relation Men-World, i.e. *transformations of human society.*

It follows that the object of the historical sciences is *human actions of all times and places* in the degree to which *they have had or now have an importance for or an influence on the existence and structure of a human group and, implicitly thereby, an importance for or an influence on the existence and structure of the present or future human community.*

This definition includes not only collective phenomena such as the Crusades or the French Revolution, but also individual behaviour or acts like the life of Napoleon, the *Pensées* of Pascal, or the effects of St Dominic, St Francis, or even of Gracchus Babeuf. For this reason it appears useful in the illustration of two pseudo-problems often found in works dealing with historical methodology. One is that of determining the historicity of an event by virtue of its influence or its worth; the other is the problem of choosing between the effects of collective forces and those of great men on history.

Concerning the problem of choosing specifically *historical* events out of the whole of reality, two opposing theories have been offered. One holds that facts are historical by virtue of the influence they exercise on the course of (subsequent) events. This was the view of Eduard Meyer, for example, to whom Max Weber replied by pointing out that, since *every happening* exercises some influence in greater or lesser degree on all others, it would be impossible to choose between historical and non-historical events. This is why Weber, rallying to the Neo-Kantian school of Heidelberg, argued that the sole criterion for this choice is the importance of events in terms of our own scale of values. An event can be historical even though it has exercised only a minimal influence on men, in so far as, for example, it expresses a fundamental human attitude towards values which still have an important relation to those which we hold today.

It can easily be seen that, if one accepts our definition, the problem becomes factitious. For, since the human community is a universal value, valid for all men, everything that has had or still has a considerable influence on the nature of this community, everything that transcends the individual and bears upon the social life (of which the intellectual life and especially values are integral parts), constitutes an historical event.

The same criterion applies to the importance of great men for the study of history. History has a single object, the social life in all its forms; and history is interested in everything that had or now has a significant influence on the community. The same is true for the life and deeds of individuals. The life of the young officer Bonaparte, had he been born fifty years earlier under Louis XV, would probably have had only an anecdotal interest in so far as circumstances would have limited his importance and his field of action. Similarly, a biography of Racine or Kierkegaard is of historical interest only to a *very limited* degree and in an *indirect way*, for whatever clarification it affords of their literary work. The literary work itself, on the other hand, is an historical fact of the highest importance by virtue of the influence which it had at a certain moment and which it still has on the modes of thought and feeling of men who constitute certain social groups. By the same token, a biography of a feudal lord of the tenth or eleventh century can be extremely interesting to an historian in so far as it exposes *typical traits* which permit the understanding of the general style of life of the nobility of that epoch or even a particularly expressive human attitude regarding certain moral and social values. On the other hand, the biography will become merely a work of erudition, more or less destitute of interest, when it deals with an individual case which is neither typical, nor expressive, and which has exercised a limited influence on the life of the groups of its time.

Thus, that which has effect on the community is, by that alone, a historical fact, for social life is the sole common value uniting all men at all times and places. What we look for in historical facts is less their material being than their *human meaning* which, obviously, cannot be known apart from their material being.

The importance of a technical or purely scholarly

study of the military techniques and procedures by which Frederick II or Napoleon, for example, won a battle resides especially in the measure to which it allows us to perceive the human and psychic energy with which these monarchs pursued their goals, the repercussions of their actions on the men of their times, and the reactions of those men; in short, everything which, by going beyond anecdotal or mere erudite detail, can establish, by means of such detail, a positive or negative human relation between ourselves and men of the past. (One could put the names of Nero or Nicholas I in place of Napoleon.)

We are here concerned with a fundamental difference between history, which studies human behaviour, and the physico-chemical sciences, which study inanimate matter. The physico-chemical sciences study facts solely in their external or sensible aspect; the historian deals with consciously realized actions (whether this consciousness be true or false) of which he must, above all, discover the *meaning*. To say that Vesuvius erupted in A.D. 79 and to look for the physical causes of that occurrence is not the same thing as to try to reconstruct the reactions of the inhabitants of Herculaneum or Pompeii to that eruption. One of the principal merits of phenomenology and of the Gestalt school of psychology has been to remind us of the importance of this distinctively human awareness and of the meanings which acts and events have for it. In this sense, to study history is first of all to try to *understand* men's actions, the impulses which have moved them, the ends which they have pursued, and the meaning which their behaviour and their actions had *for them*.

But is that all? We do not think so. The weakness of phenomenology seems to us to lie precisely in the fact that it limits itself to a comprehensive description of the facts of consciousness (or, to be more exact, of their 'essence'). The real structure of historical facts permits, however, beyond the *conscious* meaning of those facts in the thought and intentions of the actors, the postulation of an *objective* meaning which often differs from the conscious meaning in an important way.

Were the Napoleonic Wars defensive or offensive? Were they fought to establish a European hegemony or simply to defend the conquests of the Revolution against the governments of the Old Regime and, at the same time, to make England admit the existence of a new bourgeois state which could eventually become a rival? The answer depends, of course, on the result of specialized studies; but in any case these studies would have to be developed along two lines: one concentrating on the consciousness of the main actors, especially of Napoleon himself, and the other concentrating on the social, economic and political factors which rendered these wars more or less inevitable, whatever the intentions of the leaders of the Empire, and the meaning of the wars *for them*.

Similarly, the re-establishment of the dignities and titles of nobility, for example, which, according to the plan of Napoleon, were supposed to replace the old titles and to create a nobility more or less similar to the old noble class, failed to eliminate the radical and *objective* difference between the *noblesse de cour*, which was bound to the monarchy of the Old Regime, and the imperial nobility, which was objectively linked to the conquests of the Revolution (abolition of seignorial rights, sale of national holdings, the Napoleonic Code, etc.).

No historian can understand the social structure of the Empire if he ignores the subjective intention of its leaders to wipe out the last vestiges of the Jacobin

C   33 period, to re-establish social order and the nobility, and to return to legitimacy; or if he leaves unexamined its objective links with the Revolution and the struggle against the Old Regime.

Thus, the double level on which one must study historical and social events implies also a double criterion for value-judgments that must take into account both human coherency and the creative power of individuals as well as the relation between individual consciousness and objective reality. This raises one of the principal problems for any sociology of knowledge, the problem of ideologies. This problem is too vast to be studied exhaustively here, but it remains none the less at the centre of this work, as it is at the centre of every sociological study which seeks to grasp the essential aspects of human life.

METHOD IN THE HUMAN SCIENCES

The Problem of Ideologies; Material Facts and Doctrines

On the one hand, the historical and human sciences are not, like the physico-chemical sciences, the study of a collection of facts *external* to men or of a world *upon which* their action bears. On the contrary, they are the study *of this action itself*, of its structure, of the aspirations which enliven it and the changes that it undergoes. On the other hand, since consciousness is only one *real*, but *partial* aspect of human activity, historical study does not have the right to limit itself to conscious phenomena; it must connect the conscious intentions of the actors of history to the *objective* meaning of their behaviour and actions.

Two consequences follow from this.

(*a*) When it is a question of studying human life, *the process of scientific knowing, since it is itself a human, historical and social fact,* implies the *partial identity of the subject and the object of knowledge.* For this reason the problem of objectivity is posed quite otherwise in the human sciences than in physics or chemistry.

(*b*) Since human behaviour is a total reality,[1] the efforts to separate its 'material' and 'spiritual' aspects can be at best only provisory abstractions always involving great dangers for knowledge. For this reason the investigator must always strive to recover the total and concrete reality, even if he is able to succeed only in a *partial and limited* manner. He must seek to *integrate into the study of social facts the history of the theories about these facts,* and, in addition, *try to link the study of the facts of consciousness to their historical localization and to their economic and social infrastructure.*

The thorough study of these two fundamental principles of method in the human sciences would go far beyond the bounds of this work. Nevertheless we must examine them briefly, if only in a schematic manner.

i

Born in the closing years of the nineteenth century, after the works of Saint-Simon, Comte and Spencer, which were programmes rather than concrete research, non-Marxist sociology culminated in the works of E. Durkheim, the Durkheimians and, in Germany, Max Weber.

Now it seems to us that the notion of objectivity, found in these thinkers' works was inadequate because they made it depend solely on the intelligence, the individual perspicuity and the honesty of the thinker, disregarding the identity of subject and object in the human sciences and its consequences for their nature and methods. It is the merit of Max Weber's most important student, Georg Lukács (who became a Marxist later on), to have posed this problem clearly.

Our approach will take as its point of departure the three main works which have dealt with the problem in the twentieth century: E. Durkheim, *Les règles de la méthode sociologique* (*The Rules of Sociological Method*); Max Weber, *Gesammelte Aufsätze zur Wissenschaftslehre* (*Studies in the Theory of Science*); and G. Lukács, *Geschichte und Klassenbewusstsein* (*History and Class Consciousness*). First of all, let us

note that in attempting to elaborate a scientific sociology, Durkheim, and especially his disciples,[2] distinguished between two principles (already contained
implicitly in Marx's work) which today form a
definitive acquisition for any serious study.

(a) The *scientific* study of human facts, *by itself
alone*, cannot *logically establish* any value-judgment.
As Poincaré formulated it: premises in the indicative
have no *logical* conclusion in the imperative. The
'technical' utility of the social sciences resides solely
in the establishment of hypothetical imperatives (relations between certain means and certain ends) and
in the explication of the consequences implied by
adherence to certain values.

(b) The researcher must attempt to arrive at an
adequate description of the facts, avoiding any distortion due to his personal sympathies or antipathies.

On these two points, which are true moreover of
any science, there is no difference between the positions of Durkheim, Weber and Lukács. We will consider them as secured and not return to them again in
the course of the present work.

If these two points are granted, however, the problem of objectivity in the human sciences still remains
in all its amplitude.

Durkheim, it is true, seems to believe that the recognition of these two points suffices to assure the objectivity of research. He insists that the sociologist
study social facts 'as things', 'from the outside', but
never asks himself if that is *epistemologically* possible.
Let us begin by citing an example taken from the first
few pages of his book. To show the danger of preconceptions, Durkheim writes: 'The very absence of
definition sometimes causes it to be said that democracy is encountered alike at the beginning and at
the end of history. The truth is that primitive

democracy and the democracy of today are very different from each other' (p. 38). This remark is obviously aimed at Marxist analyses of primitive democracy in classless societies. (Actually, these analyses did not at all ignore the differences of which Durkheim speaks; rather, since their object was to stress the historical character of social classes, they accentuated those traits shared by primitive societies and socialist society: democracy, absence of social classes, etc.). Perhaps Durkheim was right on this particular point,[3] but three pages earlier he proposes a definition of crime as an example of 'objective definition': 'We note the existence of a certain number of acts all manifesting this external characteristic, that, once performed, they evoke from society this particular reaction called pain. We regard them as a group *sui generis*, to which we give a common name; we call any punished act a crime, and we make crime thus defined the object of a special science, criminology' (p. 35).

It should be pointed out that this definition includes acts as different as the deed of Jesus driving the money-changers from the temple, the activity of Thomas Münzer, Karl Marx or Lenin, on the one hand, and, on the other, the latest hold-up or murder; bestial acts which are as opposed to one another at least as much as primitive democracy is opposed to socialist democracy.

Yet one ought not to see this merely as an individual failing of the Durkheimian analyses, a 'contradiction', as the sociologist said to whom we pointed out the matter. This would be superficial. The two propositions are *perfectly coherent* from the *conservative* perspective in which all of Durkheim's sociology is implicity elaborated and which allows us to explain a great many other features of both his work and that of his disciples.[4] It is natural that a *conservative* sociology should see clearly the logical weaknesses of revolutionary argumentation and, in turn, commit the same *logical errors* when it is a question of defending its own values. However, from the scientific point of view the two passages cited do not have the same value.

According to Durkheim, the intrusion of value-judgments into sociological research is a weakness due simply to the youth of this science in comparison to mathematics and the physico-chemical sciences. Speaking of his fundamental rule – to treat social facts as things – he writes: 'The rule requires that the sociologist assume the same state of mind as physicists, chemists and physiologists when they get involved in a still unexplored area of their scientific domain ... But sociology is far from having arrived at this degree of intellectual maturity' (p. xiv).

In reality we know today that the difference between the working conditions of 'physicists, chemists and physiologists' and those of sociologists or historians is not one of degree but of kind; at the start of physical or chemical research there is a real and implicit agreement among all classes which make up modern society on the value, the nature and the goal of this research. The most adequate and efficacious understanding of physical and chemical reality is an ideal which today no longer offends either the interests or the values of any social class.[5] In this case, the want of objectivity in the work of a scientist can be due only to *personal* defects (*esprit de système*, lack of penetration, impassioned character, vanity and, at worst, lack of intellectual honesty).

In the human sciences, on the other hand, the situation is different. For if adequate understanding of the facts does not establish *logically* the validity of value-judgments, it is certain none the less that psychologically it favours or discredits this validity in men's consciousness. The assimilation of the category of the revolutionary to that of the criminal naturally turns the reader against the former; the existence of a classless society in primitive times renders more plausible the assertion that men might be able to construct another classless society in the future; an adequate analysis of antagonisms between the social classes in contemporary society might have unfavourable consequences for conservative ideologies, etc. In short, as regards the principal problems which confront the human sciences, the interests and the values of the social classes diverge completely. Instead of the implicit or explicit unanimity of value-judgments about the research and the adequate understanding which are found at the basis of the physio-chemical sciences, we encounter, in the human sciences, fundamental differences of attitude existing at the start, prior to the work of research, which often remain implicit and unconscious. This is why objectivity is here no longer a simple, individual problem; it is no longer merely a question of intelligence, penetration, intellectual honesty and other qualities or defects of the individual. Undoubtedly the individual can transcend the horizon of his class and accept points of view which correspond to the interests and values of another class if this new position permits him better to understand the facts; he may even – the individual not necessarily being consistent – preserve old values and acknowledge truths which are unfavourable to them. But those are relatively rare exceptions, and usually the thinker accepts, in completely good faith, the implicit categories of a mentality which, from the start, shuts him off from the understanding of an important part of reality. After this, on essential points, his intelligence, his penetration and his intellectual good faith will only accentuate and render more plausible and more tempting a distorted and ideological view of the facts.[6]

In the human sciences then it does not suffice, as Durkheim believed, to apply the Cartesian method, to call into question acquired truths and to open one's mind entirely to the facts, because the researcher generally approaches the facts with categories and implicit and unconscious preconceptions which close off to him in advance the way to an objective understanding.

The Cartesian optimism of Durkheim, his relative insensitivity to the problem of ideologies, expressed the optimistic tradition of a bourgeoisie which had been disturbed but relatively little by the development of a proletariat capable of setting over against it its own socialist vision.

Now, in the same era the situation of the German bourgeoisie was very different. In its past was an abortive revolution; in its present, an actual brutal domination. Lacking a revolutionary and humanistic tradition, it was already being threatened by a developed and organized industrial proletariat, led by a Socialist party older and more powerful than its French counterpart and which had become the world centre of theoretical Marxism, owing to the personal influence of Marx and Engels. The echoes of socialist thought and action penetrated even into university circles, which were no longer able to preserve their naïve optimism and which were obliged (at least such was the case among the most important and most honest thinkers) to take account of the facts and the new ideas that had appeared in the opposition camp. This is what explains, in great part at least, the importance of Marx's work for Max Weber, whose conservative convictions were explicit; and it also explains the fact that the latter – the most important representative of German academic sociology – consciously envisaged several problems which did not exist for Durkheim.[7]

Weber, a disciple of the Heidelberg Neo-Kantians, Rickert and Windelband, intimately acquainted with the work of Lask, which he cites several times, and whose influence he felt, was aware of the fact that if science cannot logically deny or confirm any value-judgment, neither can it completely eliminate these judgments from the work of research in the human sciences. Hence, for him, it was no longer a question of suppressing every preconception and value-judgment but, on the contrary, of consciously integrating them into science and making of them useful instruments in the search for objective truth.

In order to succeed in this undertaking, Weber rallied to the viewpoint of the Neo-Kantian school of Heidelberg. The difference between the physico-chemical sciences and the historical sciences is not, or at least not only, a matter of a difference between their objects. Above all, it is a matter of difference of perspective. The first seek general laws; the second aspire to an objective, *explicative* and *comprehensive* study of physical individuals and historical and social individualities. Now, a *historical individuality is a reality which is not given, but constructed from the given*. No science ever interprets reality in an exhaustive way. It *constructs* its object by a choice which preserves the essential and eliminates the non-essential. For the physico-chemical sciences the essential is that which recurs and can be incorporated into a system of general laws. For the human sciences, the historical individuality is constructed by the choice of what is essential *for us*, i.e. in terms of our value-judgments. Thus, historical reality changes from epoch to epoch with modifications in the hierarchy of values. It is evident that the choice bears not only on the conglomerations of facts (French Revolution, Hundred Years' War, etc.), but also, and above all, on the elements in these conglomerations which are essential or important *for us* (personalities of leaders, mass movements, intellectual matters, etc.).

Weber's basic idea is that value-judgments intervene only in the *choice* and *construction* of the object; thereafter, it becomes possible to study it in a manner that is objective and free of value-judgments, since the eliminated elements are negligible (the origin of the instrument with which Caesar was assassinated, etc.).

It seems to us unnecessary to emphasize the erroneous nature of this illusion. It goes without saying that the elements selected determine in advance the result of the study. Since these values are not 'ours', those of our culture or society, but those of this or that social class, what one perspective will eliminate as inessential may be very important from another. Moreover, Weber always speaks of what is inessential or negligible. Now there are also elements of reality essential to the existence of a class which it is not in the interests of that class to have subjected to public, or even scientific, scrutiny. Anyone seeking to study such elements will encounter powerful internal and external resistances.

On this point the thought of Max Weber is patently untenable. Although he was too rigorous a thinker to tolerate, in principle, confused or eclectic solutions – Weber always contended that he delimited in a rigorous fashion the area in which value-judgments are constitutive and those in which they must be eliminated[8] – his position is located halfway between

43

the misconception of social determinism in the thought of the Durkheimians and its integral acceptance among the Marxists.

When Weber's last essay on this subject appeared in 1919, Georg Lukács, who had become a Marxist in the meantime, had already partially written his work devoted especially to the conditions and nature of knowledge in the human sciences: *Geschichte und Klassenbewusstsein.*

In discussing the work, a true encyclopedia of the human sciences, we will restrict ourselves for the moment to the single problem which interests us here, that of *objectivity*. Lukács accepts the full consequences of the social determinism of all thought and makes of it the general law of human knowledge. For him, since all thought is by its nature intimately related to action, we may no longer legitimately speak of a 'science' of society or of sociology. The knowledge that a being has of itself is not science but *consciousness*. There is no such thing as a conservative sociology on the one hand and a dialectical sociology on the other, but only a consciousness of class, bourgeois or proletarian, which expresses itself on the level of description or explication of human events. Yet that does not lead to a universal relativism because – we will return to the matter further on – it is possible to grant the existence of a universal truth in the *consciousness horizon* (*conscience limite*) of the revolutionary proletariat, which tends to abolish all classes, to identify itself with Humanity and, above all, to wipe out every difference between the subject and object of social action, that action of which any thought is only a partial aspect.[9]

Today Lukács has rejected this excessive idealism which he himself characterizes as apocalyptic. It is unnecessary therefore to raise once more the objections to his thesis that he himself has raised. Let us simply bear in mind the following: (1) Since all historical or sociological thought is subject to profound social influences of which the individual researcher is not usually aware, it is not then a question of suppressing these influences but of rendering them explicit and integrating them into scientific research so as to avoid or reduce their distorting effect to a minimum. (2) This being the case, it is clear that there is a need for a sociological study of the social sciences themselves and, more precisely, of a materialist and dialectical study of dialectical materialism.

ii

If we compare the non-Marxist sociology of the first thirty years of our century – the sociology of Durkheim, Mauss and Weber – with that of today, we are struck by an important change in both spirit and methods.

Georges Gurvitch has shown that Durkheim – fortunately for his work, we believe – did not rigorously hold to the fundamental principle of his own method, i.e. 'to treat social facts as things'. Marcel Mauss also abandons this principle when he speaks of an irrational mode of understanding social life. In reality, behind these inconsistencies lies the problem of ideologies and value-judgments.[10]

Nevertheless, Durkheim's formula had a certain merit. Too good a sociologist himself to treat social facts 'from the outside', 'as things', his formula was expressive of a tendency – such often happens – that was destined to become increasingly predominant in the United States, as in Europe, down to the present. If the works of the Durkheimians and those of Max Weber are compared with the majority of contemporary non-dialectical sociological works, however, the difference between them is obvious. First of all, because of the general method used, works like *Les formes élémentaires de la vie religieuse* (*The Elementary Forms of Religious Life*) by Durkheim, *La classe ouvrière et les niveaux de vie* (*The Working Class and the Standards of Living*) by Halbwachs, *Essai sur le Don* (*The Gift*) by Mauss, *La foi jurée* (*The Sworn Trust*) by Davy, and *Die protestantische Ethik und der Geist des Kapitalismus* (*The Protestant Ethic and the Spirit of Capitalism*) by Weber, are all as rich in concrete empirical data as in general explanatory theories.[11] But as Nels Anderson writes in a survey article which is *very favourable* to contemporary American sociology : 'If a group of social researchers assembles, rarely do they discuss many social theories, certainly as compared with methodology ... those who are preoccupied most with the present problems of research seem to be preoccupied least with theoretical analyses. That does not mean that theory is neglected by contemporary sociology. It seems rather that theory is of more interest to those sociologists who are not very much concerned with research.'[12] This situation is also characteristic of most representative European work. One need only read the writings of Gurvitch and L. von Wiese or peruse the articles of the great theoretical reviews to become aware of it. We will return to this matter further on.

As for concrete research, a profound transformation in methods has occurred since the classical period. New procedures have been discovered; others have come to the fore. Inquiries, monographs, statistics, microsociology, sociometry, etc. – these new methods share above all the characteristic of effectively having realized the Durkheimian ideal of treating the external facts 'as things' analogous to the objects of the physical sciences. Yet is the information about reality which they offer us more objective? The issue seems debatable to us because, in the majority of cases, the partisans of these methods, which may be grouped under the term descriptive, have already, even before beginning their work, taken a stand *for the present social order*, which they consider natural and normal and which no longer seems to them even to require a justification. But so long as it is not *inserted into a comprehensive analysis and does not embrace a long historical period*, no inquiry, no monograph – *whatever its usefulness as an investigation* – will be able to utilize as evidence the forces conducing to the transformation and renovation in a society, especially as the effect of these forces often accumulates over long periods of time without their external manifestations being easily noted. Social reality is a total reality. Like international treaties, monographic findings and the results of any inquiry are valid only as long as *rebus sic stantibus*; thus it is a question of those 'things' which are important to the sociologist.

An inquiry about royalty among the French peasants or artisans of the Faubourg Saint-Antoine in 1789; another among the Russian peasants in January 1917, would have produced results quite different from those of a similar inquiry made a year later. Now this rapid change in the two cases would have been the result of a secular transformation which probably would have escaped the notice of any empirical (*extérieure*) monograph in the style sanctioned by the majority of sociologists today. For the facts recorded by a monograph or an inquiry only achieve their valid signification within the context of a comprehensive vision which knows how to approach them and extract the human content they conceal.

It is necessary to go further however. The data as

47

such also depend on the conscious or implicit vision of the inquirer. There are no brute facts. No inquiry, no monograph is ever exhaustive. *It only asks certain questions of reality and chooses the facts in the light of these questions*. Moreover, in the image that it constructs, the importance given to the different facts that it accepts for recording is proportional to what the problems represent for the researcher or investigator. Thus there is always a set purpose, a collection of preconceptions that decide:

(*a*) which questions may and may not be asked of reality:

(*b*) the importance to be given to the different factors in which an interest is taken.

Now in all this it is a question of factors which are usually implicit and which invalidate in advance a good many would-be objective works.

Let us add that microsociology in general, and sociometry in particular, which may offer a limited, but indisputable usefulness,[13] *on condition they are framed within a comprehensive vision*, become distorting as soon as they attempt to comprehend – and this is most frequently the case – relations between the individuals who compose a partial collectivity (such as a scholarly class, factory or village) outside of essential social groups (such as social classes and nations) and antagonisms, balances or collaborations between them.

Up to now we have treated in a general manner the preconceptions which are implicit in contemporary sociology. The gravity of the situation becomes manifest when certain concrete examples are considered.

Thus Anderson, in the article already cited, speaks with somewhat disconcerting praise of contemporary American sociologists: 'Despite the multiple forms of social research,' he writes, 'and the multiple and varied utilization of information obtained with the aid of this research, the majority of researchers allow themselves to be guided by good (*sauber*) intentions. They have become competent advisors to business concerns, political parties, benevolent associations or public administrations' (p. 68). We could not imagine a franker, more open recognition of the social foundations of such research. One can only ask oneself, with a certain disquietude, about the activity of other sociologists whose preoccupations are not 'good'.

Elsewhere R. König, professor of sociology at the universities of Zürich and Cologne, defines sociology as 'a factor in the process of the social autodomestication of humanity'.[14] For him the essential problem of sociology is the adaptation of individuals to existing society, and not that of historical crises and progress. Proposing a conception of 'permanent revolution' in order to 'neutralize' real revolution (p. 92) he writes that: 'Today it can be stated unequivocally that the "10 points" of the "Communist Manifesto" are not only realized in essence but that modern social politics has provided a great deal more security for labour than Marx ever dreamed possible. This statement is, perhaps, not so valid (*nicht so sehr*) for the Soviet Union, but is indeed for the Western progressive democracies' (p. 39).

Let us merely add that among the '10 points' there are the abolition of the right of inheritance and the nationalization of land and that, in 1949, the date when the statement cited appeared, a large number of the workers of France, Italy and Germany were hardly able to support themselves decently.

In one of the great German sociological journals, W. Mitze published an article entitled 'Youth and Proletariat' in which he explains that the plight of the

D

proletariat is not the result of an economic situation but of an unhealthy psychic imbalance. Let us cite at random some lines of this article which seem scarcely to require any comment.[15]

'The condition of the proletariat is nothing more than a problem of attitude, that is to say, a negative psychological attitude, allied to what generally is considered typical of a certain phase in the adolescent's development with its continual negations' (p. 48). 'Hence one could justly conclude that it is not so much poverty in itself which makes a proletarian of a man but rather the way in which he reacts to the state of poverty' (p. 49). 'The proof' that a healthy psychological attitude is all that is required to rise from the proletariat is found, among other things, in 'an upward social mobility of German families, which has been going on for dozens of years. What we still find today as depressed in each people is this hereditary proletariat which no longer interests anyone, outside of organizations for social assistance and eugenists, namely degenerate families from which are recruited vagabonds, criminals, drunkards and a-social types' (p. 40). Finally, in making references to Tumlirz, Mitze cites as proof of the possibility of social mobility through a positive psychological attitude the fact that 'the proletarian consciousness is alien to wholesome and attractive girls of the lower classes. For every girl hopes to rise socially by means of her physical attributes' (p. 48).

We could go on at length. It will be better, however, to return to the problem which concerns us.

iii

Once the conscious or unconscious effect of value-judgments on scientific theories is recognized, the problem of the *criterion of truth* is raised. Must a sociology of knowledge lead to relativism? Are all ideologies of equal value, at least, as far as the search for truth is concerned; and is the choice of one over another only a matter of individual preference?

The most important sociologists of knowledge have not thought so. We have already noted the positions of Durkheim and Weber, which seem to us inadequate. In 1918 Georg Lukács referred to a reality-horizon (*réalité limite*) which seemed at that time to be near realization or even already present. This was contained in the *potential consciousness* (*conscience possible*) of the revolutionary proletariat which sought to abolish all classes and to identify itself with society as a whole, thereby creating a situation in which the thinker could identify himself with human consciousness in general, that is, *with both the subject and the object* of the social sciences, and which would be in fact the realization of the absolute spirit of Hegel.[16] Today we know (even Lukács knows it) that this reality-horizon, far from being present, was almost an apocalyptical vision. In any case, for us it has value primarily as an ideal concept, not as a practical reality.

Subsequently, Karl Mannheim has simplified the problem by substituting for Lukács's position a veritable plea of defence *pro domo*. In place of the limited consciousness of the revolutionary proletariat, he has discovered an actual group which presumably enjoys a privileged position that permits it to achieve an adequate knowledge of reality. This group is the '*freischwebende Intelligenz*', a term which might be rendered as 'free-floating intelligentsia'. In effect, Mannheim's position boiled down to making truth once again the perquisite of a certain number of scholars and specialists in sociology. It is not surprising that his work was favourably received and that he has

been seen as the 'creator' of the sociology of knowledge.[17]

It is, however, difficult to see how intellectuals, since
they express in their work not only the thought
of other groups but also their own *social character as
intellectuals* could possess a less subjective point of
view than that of any other professional group, such
as lawyers, priests, shoemakers or the like. Intellectuals, like other groups, belong to a social class, to a
nation, and so on; and they have their own individual,
particular and general economic interests.

To us Mannheim's work seems to be important less
as a step forward in the sociology of knowledge (whatever is valuable in it was already present in Lukács's
Geschichte und Klassenbewusstsein, which inspired it)
than as a passionate reaffirmation of the basic precepts
of this sociology.

The inadequacy of the solutions of Durkheim,
Weber, Lukács and Mannheim having been indicated,
we may now state that, to us, the proper solution lies
in a synthesis of two types of considerations:

(1) Viewed in terms of their effect on scientific
thought, *different perspectives and ideologies do not
exist on the same plane.* Some value-judgments permit
a better understanding of reality than others. When
it is a question of determining which of two con-
flicting sociologies has the greater scientific value, the
first step is to ask which of them *permits the understanding of the other as a social and human phenomenon, reveals its infrastructure, and clarifies, by
means of an immanent critical principle, its inconsistencies and its limitations.*

By way of illustrating this criterion, let us cite an
example already mentioned in another context, Gurvitch's analysis of the relation between the thought of
Saint-Simon and the thought of Marx.[18] The influence

of the former on the latter is undeniable. Engels had already pointed it out. However, the relationship does not seem as close to us as it does to Gurvitch. Saint-Simon analysed with extraordinary precision the historical importance of the class struggle between the bourgeoisie and the feudal nobility, a struggle which had dominated French history since the twelfth century. He perceived the de facto alliance between the Third Estate and the monarchy up to the time of Louis XIV and the change in the policy of the monarchy, which, after Louis XIV's reign, came to rely increasingly on the nobility as a counterweight to a Third Estate whose power was continually growing. It was possible for Saint-Simon to produce a correct analysis, in its general lines, of these phenomena, for he was a thinker who wrote – consciously moreover – from the viewpoint of the Third Estate, of industrialists and merchants, and who saw in the restored Bourbon monarchy merely a *possible* ally or a *possible* enemy. But precisely because he saw everything from this viewpoint, Saint-Simon was never able to comprehend or even to envisage the possibility of antagonism between the proletariat and the bourgeoisie. The agreement, and even the identity of interests, of these two classes constituted for him an implicit postulate, a manifest truth which it was unnecessary to discuss or to prove. He clearly perceived a certain number of problems which confronted the working class : misery, unemployment, etc., but he saw only one solution to these problems : the seizure of political power by the industrialists.

(2) On the other hand, Marx sees the struggle between the proletariat and the bourgeoisie as the keystone of contemporary social life and, at the same time, as the great hope of humanity, the force which must ultimately bring about socialism.

Limiting ourselves to the purely scientific plane, which of these positions offers a better understanding of reality? By choosing that of Marx we can establish the validity of an important argument. From his point of view, we are able to understand the Saint-Simonian ideology as a social fact, its infrastructure and its limitations; we are even able to understand Marxism itself, as the ideology of the proletariat. Since the interests of the proletariat and those of the industrialists were identical for Saint-Simon, any attempt to envisage a possible opposition between them could be for him only demagogy, the work of agitators, etc.

The difference between the kind of sociology postulated by us and that found in many contemporary 'objective' sociological studies is exactly the same. We can very well understand the infrastructure of this kind of sociology, the partial but none the less real usefulness of its concrete investigations, and why its possibilities of understanding social life grow progressively narrow under the influence of aggravations attending the class struggle which put into question the very existence of the bourgeois world. By contrast, the 'objective' sociologists of today succeed less than ever in understanding Marxist thought as a social and human fact and are unable to discuss seriously, in the light of concrete facts, its truth, error or partial limitation. They are content to criticize Marxism, in a general and abstract manner, for its 'eschatological' character, or its 'one-sided' and 'narrow' point of view. They distort the thought of Marx and Engels, thereby creating an imaginary opponent easier to combat, or else they suggest that Marx, if he had known such and such a fact, would not have been a Marxist. There are numerous examples of which we will cite only a few.

Sorokin writes, in all seriousness, that Engels 'identifies social class with unifunctional social groups' and includes him among those thinkers for whom a social class is a 'professional, racial, linguistic, etc., group'.[19] As for Marx himself, we are told that 'he never developed a sufficiently clear conception of social class.' Among the 'Marxists', Sorokin deals at length with Bukharin. First he gives Bukharin's definition of social class: 'a collection of persons who play the same role in production *and* [italics mine] who maintain the same relations of production with other persons participating in the productive process'.[20] He then raises an objection to Bukharin's definition which is, to say the least, surprising: 'It is not at all correct', writes Sorokin, 'to say that all persons playing the same role in the productive process receive a wage and share similar psycho-social and cultural characteristics'.[21] Is it necessary to add that if Bukharin had believed this for a moment, the second half of his sentence would not have been necessary, and that he added it *precisely* in order to avoid a definition which is made too restricted in comprehension and too broad in extension if limited only to 'role in production'?

Gurvitch transforms the difference in emphasis and preoccupation, which undeniably exists between the writings of the young Marx and those of his mature period, into a fundamental opposition. Grouping the youthful writings of Marx with those of Proudhon and Saint-Simon, Gurvitch contrasts them with a so-called 'dogmatism' of the second period, all of this on a wholly abstract and dogmatic level and without the slightest reference to the infrastructure of Marxist thought or to the social facts which Marx was trying to explain. It is in relation to these facts, if at all, that Marx's 'dogmatism' should have been demonstrated!

J. L. Moreno, without any supporting argument whatsoever, tells us that (sociometric) 'super-selection' is analogous to the surplus value observed by Marx.

According to Moreno: 'A change in the image of the phenomenon of profit in economic relations reflects a change in the image of selections on the interpersonal and intergroup level. The social revolution, considered as the final moment of the class struggle, constitutes an error in sociological interpretation ... It would be extremely interesting to see how Marx – had he taken this new aspect of the problems into account – would have altered his theory of social revolution. *In any case*, [italics mine] it seems that he might have attributed revolutionary action not only to the great social units, but also to the smallest, to the social atoms, those primary centres of attraction and repulsion capable of rendering the revolution truly effective and permanent.'[22] Similarly, we read near the end of Gurvitch's study of Marx that 'in order to maintain the extremely fruitful and subtle point of view of his early sociology, Marx *would have had* [italics mine] to push his *sociological relativism* even further.[23] He would have had to recognize that the relations between the levels and strata of social reality distinguished by him were themselves variable, and that their position in the hierarchy, as dynamic forces of change, switched constantly according to the type of society in question ... ' Only thus would he 'have been able to avoid the trap of "economic determinism" into which he ultimately fell.'[24] Have not Moreno and Gurvitch, in the guise of critics of his thought, simply criticized Marx for not sharing their point of view, which 'in any case' he would have been 'forced' to adopt ... if he had not been Marx?

Thus, the possibility of choosing, from among the different world-views, the one which provides the widest possible form and range of comprehension, already constitutes an important step towards an adequate knowledge of the truth. It is also true, however, that even this perspective can, in principle and usually in fact, contain two kinds of limitations.

(a) There are those which derive from the fact that certain aspects of reality, visible from a reactionary point of view, which is almost always more limited and narrow, are not visible from the standpoint of the ascending class. The most typical case we know of is Pascal's critique of Cartesian rationalism and the hope of a universal mathematics, a criticism which remained incomprehensible from the point of view of the Third Estate in the seventeenth century.

(b) There are limitations which prevent even possible consciousness in the broadest sense from making the adjustment of truth to reality, and which, since they are implicit and unconscious in the individual thinker, reveal themselves only progressively, in the light of the subsequent evolution of history. Are there no means available for transcending these limitations? Before ending this section, we think it necessary to take account of a factor which is of *undeniable* importance in research but which sociologists of knowledge have in general left unexamined heretofore: this factor is the individual.

We are not speaking of the group of intellectuals as such, the '*freischwebende Intelligenz*' of Mannheim, but of the individual pure and simple, whether he be an intellectual, worker, artisan or bourgeois. Can the individual get beyond the limits of the potential consciousness of the group, whose perspective is larger and more variegated? Frankly, we do not know. The problem is purely theoretical. We have never encountered it in the course of our concrete research, and if there were such individuals, their thought would have inevitably remained obscure and without influence; at best a later thinker might rediscover and value them as precursors of a point of view which only subsequently became a social and spiritual reality. A writer who might have supported the idea of a centralized state in the tenth century, another who might have perceived the influence of economics on religious life in the fifteenth and sixteenth centuries, or a thinker who, in the seventeenth century, might have foreseen the class struggle between the proletariat and the bourgeoisie – all of these would be cases in point.

But for the moment we want to deal with a phenomenon which is important in a different way for history and the development of the human sciences. It is possible for the individual, if he realizes certain conditions, which are always *exceptional*, to arrive, in the realm of scientific thought, at a kind of knowledge which goes beyond the real consciousness of all social classes actually existing at the time in which he is living. He can do this by: (a) effecting a synthesis of the elements of truth provided by the perspectives of several different social classes; and (b) by preserving the elements of understanding already expressed earlier by this or that thinker but later abandoned under the influence of social, economic and political changes.

Before analysing this possibility, let us say immediately that it is much more important for *scientific thought* than for philosophical or literary works in which every attempt at synthesis between opposed world-views leads to a lack of coherence and to eclecticism. The scientist must understand reality to the fullest; this is the *sole* legitimate criterion for judging the value of his work. And if, in order to do this, he must deal with a totality of facts which *none* of the existing world-views can explain, his work poses a problem for philosophers which they will be able to resolve only later, when history has created social conditions favourable to that solution.

On the subject of the relations between the individual and the class, we wrote two years ago that: 'Without conceiving thought and consciousness as metaphysical entities, divorced from the rest of individual and social life, it is obvious that the freedom of the thinker and writer differs greatly from that of other persons; their ties with the life of society are diversely complex and mediatized in different ways; the internal logic of their work is autonomous in different ways, to a much greater extent than any abstract and mechanistic sociology has ever been willing to admit ... Undoubtedly, the thinking of an individual can be influenced in many ways by the environment with which he has been in immediate contact; however, this influence can produce different effects: as an adaptation but also a reaction of refusal or rebellion, or even as a synthesis of ideas met with in one environment with others coming from elsewhere, etc. ...

'The influence of the environment can also be opposed and even overcome by that of ideologies far removed in time and space. Be that as it may, this is a complex phenomenon which cannot be reduced to a mechanical schema.'[25]

The great *representative* writers are those who express, in a more or less coherent way, a world-view which corresponds to the maximum of possible consciousness of a class; this is the case especially for philosophers, writers and artists. For the scientist, the situation is sometimes different. His essential task is to achieve the most comprehensive knowledge of reality. Now, it is precisely the *relative* independence of the individual with respect to the group, of which we have already spoken, that permits him, in certain cases, to correct the limitations of a view with adequate knowledge which might conflict with this view

59

but be perfectly compatible with another real view of a different class. The scientist may even enlarge the limits of real consciousness of a class in a given epoch, by means of the general potential (*possibilités générales*) of this class in the totality of the historical period.

Because he exists at the centre of a particular sector of the total life of the group, that of theoretical thinking; because he is employed in the search for truth as a supreme moral value; because in the course of his work he encounters the most varied theories, each of which contains a greater or lesser part of the truth; and above all because he excels at disclosing the weaknesses of opposing theories, the scientist will, in certain indubitably exceptional cases, be able to take an important step in the direction of objective truth beyond the current limitations of the group to which he belongs.

But in order to do this, he must satisfy a complex set of conditions. We would like to examine briefly some of those which, at first glance, appear most obvious.

(1) He must not think that the difficulties of research in the human sciences, however great, are of the same order as those in the physico-chemical sciences and that the whole matter is merely a question of intelligence and good will. He must be aware of the fact that, in addition to the difficulties *common to all of the sciences*, he will be confronted here by specific difficulties deriving from the influence of the class struggle on the consciousness of men in general and on his own consciousness in particular. He must first seek to identify this influence wherever he suspects it exists.

(2) He must not hesitate to enter into conflict with the most deeply rooted prejudices, the most firmly established authorities, or those verities which ap-

pear most self-evident; and *especially* he must not fear any *orthodoxy* or any *heresy*, since the two dangers are equally great.

(3) Since the effect of the group on its own thought and on that of others is *permanent* and *continual*, he must not believe that methodical doubt, which is preliminary and bears only upon inherited notions and conscious preconceptions is sufficient. His first task should be a rigorous, and above all *permanent* and *continual*, critique of his own findings and of the progress of his own thought. This critical attitude has to become a natural predisposition, a second nature, to use Pascal's phrase.

There is no effective weapon for suppressing implicit preconceptions once and for all. This is a difficult struggle, which must be renewed every day and which, at some point, makes manifest the importance of the fundamental elements of the dialectical method in the human sciences.

(4) In order to understand and evaluate all positions, his own as well as others, he must relate them both to *their social infrastructures*, so as to understand their meaning, and *to the facts they purport* to explain or describe; only thus can he extract the element of truth which they contain.

Let us add that, when he has fulfilled all of these conditions to the limit of his possibilities – not to mention those which are common to scientific work in general (precision, elimination of all personal considerations, etc.) –, when he has brought to bear his critical spirit upon his own position and tried to correct it wherever his own reflections or the criticism of his opponents has revealed to him his weaknesses and distortions, when he has thus achieved the impression that he has succeeded in inserting his own thought into concrete social reality, he will find himself in the general position of the man of science. He will have discovered a number of approximative truths valuable until such time as the researchers who will come after him continue and go beyond his own work.

All of this should show the importance of the clarification of ideologies for the establishment of a scientific method in the historical and social sciences. It remains to stress some of the elements which constitute this method and which make possible the struggle against distortions resulting from the effect of implicit preconceptions.

iv

After this schematic outline of the problem of objectivity in the historical, social and human sciences, we arrive at the second major methodological principle, that of the *total* character of human activity and the indissoluble bond between the history of economic and social facts and the history of ideas.

This principle is axiomatic for dialectical thought, but it has been generally ignored by non-Marxist social science. The dialectical method is always *genetic* and, like every human reality, is both *material* and *psychic*: the genetic study of a human fact implies in every case and in the same degree its material history and the history of the doctrines which concern it. There is nothing more curious than the lament, constantly reiterated by opponents of Marxism, that it neglects the realm of ideas and the spiritual life. One of the basic theses of the Marxist method is that any serious study of human reality leads back to thought when its material aspect has been taken of the point of departure and to social and economic reality when one has begun with the history of ideas. One need only recall the organization of the majority of the great classic works of Marxism. A large part of *Das Kapital (Capital)* was to have been made up of those writings of Marx published posthumously by Kautsky under the title *Theorien über den Mehrwert (Theories of Surplus Value)*; a good third of *Die Akkumulation des Kapitals (The Accumulation of Capital)* by Rosa Luxemburg is devoted to the history of theories of accumulation; in Lenin's *Gosudarstvo i Revolutsia (State and Revolution)*, the analysis of the structure of the state is inseparable from the history of revolutionary theories involving the state; and also, in Lukács's *Geschichte und Klassenbewusstsein*, the analysis of the facts and the history of economic, social and philosophical doctrines are inextricably bound up one with the other.

Undoubtedly it will be objected that many non-Marxist works devote some attention to the history of ideas; but, as Lukács observed, there is usually a *fundamental* difference between these works and dialectical ones. In non-dialectical works, the chapters devoted to theory in sociological and historical studies, and conversely, the chapters devoted to social and historical reality in histories of ideas or of literature and the arts, are treated as extraneous bodies; they are usually inspired by an interest in pure erudition or offered merely in the interest of general information. For the dialectical thinker, however, doctrines form the integrating part of the social reality itself and can be detached from it only by makeshift abstractions; the study of them is an *indispensable* element of the effective study of the problem in the same way that social and historical reality constitutes one of the most important elements for understanding the spiritual life of an age. For the dialectical thinker, the history of philosophy is an element and an aspect of the philosophy of history; the history of a problem is one of the aspects of the problem itself and of history in general; and the arm of criticism, as Marx put it, is a step towards criticism by arms.

Let us take some examples at random. How is it possible to understand credit or the family apart from their genesis, and how can we separate the study of this genesis from the evolution of theories concerning the legitimacy of interest, the sin of usury, marriage and family life? Or to take two examples from our own research : It is clear that the philosophy of Kant and that of Pascal are more comprehensible if they are related to their social infrastructures, but it is just as obvious that these same infrastructures are more easily understood if they are related to, among other things, the thought of these two philosophers. And, moreover, both are more easily understood if contrasted, on the one hand, with the individualistic doctrines which preceded them and their infrastructures and, on the other hand, with the different interpretations of succeeding eras and the economic and social conditions which have influenced and usually determined them. Kant becomes more comprehensible if viewed as the philosopher of the tragic situation of the eighteenth-century German bourgeoisie, which aspired to a revolution that it was unable to bring about; especially if one opposes this interpretation of his work to that of the nineteenth century, which we have called the 'Neo-Kantian misunderstanding', where the elimination of the thing-in-itself and of the sovereign good expressed the thought of a social stratum which, while making use of Kant's name, no longer aspired to any social transformation whatsoever.[26]

Similarly, Pascal's *Pensées* (and the tragedies of Racine) are difficult to understand apart from the social structure of France in the seventeenth century. That is to say we must understand the tragic situation of the *noblesse de robe*, torn between its bourgeois origins and ties on the one side, and, on the other, its current alliance with the monarchy, which was just beginning to disassociate itself from the Third Estate; torn consequently between its thought and its emotions. And we must understand that current of Jansenism which was the radical ideological expression of the world-view of this *noblesse de robe*, as well as the persecution of Jansenism by the Church and the monarchy. Moreover, the true significance of Pascal's thought comes to light particularly if contrasted with the rationalist interpretations of it provided by the revolutionary bourgeoisie (Condorcet, Voltaire, the distinction between the 'homme à l'amulette' and the 'homme à la roulette') of the eighteenth century; with the moderate interpretation of Vinet, who proposed to temper the 'excesses' of Pascal; and with the interpretation of Cousin, who saw Pascal as a brilliant, but dangerous and anarchical, sceptic. Both Vinet's interpretation of Pascal's thought and that of Cousin are expressions of a bourgeoisie solidly seated in power and hostile to every form of extremism. Finally, we may contrast it with the irrationalist interpretation of Shestov in the twentieth century, which is the exact opposite of the rationalist view, just as the bourgeoisie in decline is the opposite of the revolutionary bourgeoisie.

It is thus easy to understand why there have never been any disciples of Pascal in France.[27] Over the course of its three stages of ascent, power and decline, the bourgeoisie has never been able to accept this brilliant representative of a class and of an ideology which disappeared with the Old Regime.

The fruitfulness and importance of this approach could only be illustrated by a concrete analysis that would exceed the limits of this study. We shall have

E

to rest content with a schematic sketch of the evolution of sociology in the course of the last few decades.

During the last third of the nineteenth century and up to around 1930, sociology underwent a considerable development. During that time, numerous concrete studies aroused hope of an almost infinite progress. The great works of the Durkheimians in France, the sociology of knowledge in Germany (with Scheler and Mannheim), the studies of Weber, as well as those historical and economic works profoundly transformed and influenced by sociology (one need only mention Mathiez, Marc Bloch, Henri Pirenne, Lamprecht, Sombart and Troeltsch), all this brought to light a new dimension of human reality. A considerable area for the exploration and comprehension of the spiritual life was opened up, and some thinkers even came to believe that sociology had been called upon to replace the other human sciences.

Marxists, however, observed this development with a sceptical and cautious eye. And I am not speaking here of the criticism of certain theories or of the acceptance or rejection of certain concrete results of those investigations. Disagreements of this sort are part of the normal development of science and are a natural result of that freedom of thought and of criticism which are *indispensable to the progress of knowledge*. The reservations of the Marxists had to do with the future of academic sociology and its limitations for the comprehension of human reality. The importance of the social dimension in the study of that reality was discovered by bourgeois ideologues at the beginning of the nineteenth century, and academic social science began to utilize it *in a concrete manner* near the end of the nineteenth century and during the first third of the twentieth century; but it was discerned by Marx himself, who used it in his own analyses with exceptional insight as early as 1840-50.

But Marx had also demonstrated the social conditioning of the historical and social sciences themselves and the impossibility of transcending certain limitations in the understanding of human reality without transcending at the same time the framework of capitalist society and objectively serving – either consciously or unconsciously – the interests of the proletariat by this very research.

Actually, the great flowering of non-Marxist sociology corresponded to a *precise* and *limited* era in the history of the Western bourgeoisie, an era for which theorists as different as Sombart, Hilferding and Lenin felt the need for a special term (apogee of capitalism, finance capitalism, imperialism) and of which we might here list three characteristic attributes.

(a) During this period, the inadequacy of individualism and of the circumstances of free competition for the solution of economic, political and social problems became manifest to bourgeois thinkers themselves. The economic and literary fantasies, which at the beginning of the nineteenth century still marvellously expressed bourgeois thought, were surpassed towards the end of the century, not only by the systems of the doctrinaires, but also and above all by virtue of real changes in the economy and society. On the economic plane, this was the age of finance capitalism, of the cartels, and of the trusts; on the social plane it saw the political and unionist organization of the working classes; on the political plane it witnessed the exploitation of the world by the great powers. In literature, from Balzac to Zola, the figures of Goriot, Gobseck, Rastignac and Nucingen were replaced by the stock exchange, the mine, the land, the great stores, etc. In the human sciences, sociology, the science of groups, contended with individual psychology for control of the field.

(b) Despite these changes, the Western bourgeoisie still stood at the head of a vigorous and viable social order which had not yet entered into its phase of decline. Its dominance was solidly established: the socialist menace was only theoretical and remote; the policy of the workers' parties and of the trade unions was reformist (despite their apparently revolutionary ideology); collaboration between the classes in Western Europe was a reality. This is why the ideology of the bourgeois class still had, in part, real content and an effective social function, because it assured the development of the productive forces of civilization within a viable social order (even though that social order was unjust and was based on the exploitation of man by man). Thus, like every class which still performs an authentic social function, the bourgeoisie was able to understand certain essential aspects of reality.

(c) To be precise, however, it is necessary to add that the ideology of the bourgeoisie, its values and its notion of order, had become completely conservative (like the bourgeois class itself) and differed *qualitatively* from the optimistic faith of the formerly revolutionary bourgeoisie, which was confident of assuring by its acts the forward march of humanity.

The optimistic ideologues of the revolutionary and post-revolutionary bourgeoisie, such as Condorcet, Saint-Simon, Lessing and Kant, gave way to the great pessimistic thinkers, beginning with Schopenhauer, who only foreshadowed imperialism, down to Burckhardt and Thomas Mann, who express it, and Spengler, who already heralds the phase of decline. These last are all German or write in the German language. In fact, among the great countries of the West, Germany was the most unbalanced society, the most fragile and, implicitly, the most sensitive to the threats of the future.[28]

But the pessimism of these thinkers remains in the background; it is a theoretical pessimism and not a *lived* and *actual* despair. Kierkegaard remains for the time being a misunderstood and isolated eccentric. Later, Kafka died unknown and unappreciated. Only in its phase of decline will the bourgeoisie make of them, retrospectively, the great thinker and the great writer that we can see in them today. On the philosophical plane at the end of the nineteenth century, a representative thinker such as Hermann Cohen saw himself as the defender of the living spirit of Kantian thought against Kant himself, dispensing with the notion of the sovereign good because, as he put it, 'we have no need of this better world.'[29]

This complex of facts also explains both the possibilities and the limitations of academic sociology during the period under examination. It produced a certain number of concrete studies which remain a definite achievement for the social sciences, although the explanation of the social facts everywhere ran up against an insuperable barrier: the conscious or unconscious tendency to avoid any explanation based on the concept of class struggle and (given the bond between Marxism and historical materialism) a tendency, less strong, to underestimate the importance of economic factors in the understanding of human reality.

By way of example, let us take Max Weber's study of the relation between the Protestant mentality and capitalism. Weber quite naturally accepts the former as being the determinating factor, although the facts, which he brilliantly analysed, can be explained equally well by reversing his hypothesis and above all by the much more likely one of a *total human reality which expresses itself on all levels of social life.*

The Durkheimians, with the exception of two works by Halbwachs, almost never utilize the category of social class in their interpretations; and the tendency to avoid this problem is probably what led them to devote so much of their effort to the study of primitive societies, where class differentiations had not yet emerged. The same reasons, moreover, probably lie behind the paucity of information which this mass of studies of totemistic societies offers concerning their modes of production and economic life. None the less, and in spite of these limitations, the works of Max Weber, Durkheim, Mauss, Halbwachs, Lévy-Bruhl, Davy and Fauconnet represent a substantial contribution to the understanding of the social life, and to this tradition of concrete research it is undoubtedly necessary to add the work of certain thinkers who carry on their line of investigation today. For France it will be enough to mention G. Le Bras and Claude Lévi-Strauss.[30]

But neither Max Weber nor the Durkheimians had genuine continuators; the influence of Durkheim survives for the most part only in the sphere of purely ethnographic research. Between the sociology of the period 1890–1930 and what Gurvitch, in a work edited by him, calls *Twentieth Century Sociology*, there is a fundamental break, which to us seems to correspond to the philosophic break between the great period of academic rationalism and contemporary Existentialism; to the literary rupture between the last great writers of the bourgeoisie, André Gide, Thomas Mann, Roger Martin du Gard, and the great writer of our time, Franz Kafka; and especially to the economic and social transition of the Western European bourgeoisie from its phase of imperialism to its phase of decline.

Aside from certain specialists who continue the older tradition of concrete research, contemporary sociology increasingly loses contact with reality.

We have already spoken of the inadequacies of the new descriptive methods of contemporary sociology and of the separation of theory from concrete research. The common factor running through tendencies which are apparently different and even opposed, is *the radical elimination of every historical element* from the study of human facts. On the theoretical level, this gives rise to the tendency, ever more pronounced, to substitute for sociology a kind of pseudo-social psychology which distorts the facts all the more by eliminating every social and historical element from the psychological life of individuals; it seeks rather to make of the psychological life the explanatory key to mass phenomena. In the work already cited, König affirms this openly: after having explained that today it is possible to reduce Tarde and Durkheim 'to the same plane', by replacing the distinction between individual and collective representations by a 'social psychology' and the much simpler 'distinction between the contents of purely individual consciousness and those oriented towards the social (*sozialausgerichtet*)', we are told that especially the latter 'are distinguished by a certain constraint' which 'becomes at the same time a cause of their endless repetition, such that in the final analysis socio-historical reality appears as a moral relation of a specific sort' (p. 23). Thus, socio-historical reality is reduced by König to the infinite repetition of individual psychic and moral processes. It is little wonder that, in clarifying his method, he continues: 'In the same way, *the problem of crisis is lifted out of its general historico-philosophical (geschichtsphilosophisch) context* [our italics]'; it is concretized and reduced (*wird*

71

überbunden) 'to individual phenomena and precisely delimited individual situations. The decisive irreducible quantity which we will encounter at the end of our analyses will be the phenomenon of adaptation (or conversely, false or non-adaptation)' (p. 23).

The lines just cited are not, however, an individual aberration. König is simply stating, in a particularly open and clear manner, the method of sociologists as well known as von Wiese in Germany and Moreno in the United States.

On this level, as a matter of fact, von Wiese has the merit of being a pioneer. For his part, he has long since eliminated from sociology every concrete *content* of human life. For him sociology is reduced to the study of the phenomena of psychological attraction and repulsion between individuals; and we understand him very well when he prefaces his many (very favourable) reviews of contemporary works with the remark that he had already said the same thing thirty or forty years earlier.[31]

In the United States Moreno created sociometry which, basically, is an attempt to develop on the same anti-historical presuppositions as those of von Wiese a more or less 'quantitative' science (scientism always works under the superstition of the 'quantitative' and of 'measurement').[32] Moreno believes that he has found in the approach a kind of panacea capable of holding the vindictive workers' movements at bay and of solving almost every social problem. In one of his articles he writes: 'The researchers who employ socio-dramatic techniques must, to begin with, organize preventive, didactic and therapeutic meetings in the groups in which they live and work; they must organize, on demand, such meetings wherever analogous problems arise; penetrate into groups which are prey to urgent or chronic social difficulties; merge themselves in meetings organized by strikers, in rebellions of various types, in rallies and political demonstrations, etc.'[33]

'The difficulty encountered by Marxism can be summarized in a single phrase : its ignorance of the autonomous socio-dynamic structure of modern society' (p. 76). 'Sociometric experimentation aims at transforming the old social order into a new order' (p. 51). 'Like an infant, humanity only matures little by little; it is only to the degree in which a sociometric consciousness will gradually remodel our social institutions that humanity will find a social structure capable of serving as a framework for a universal society' (p. 74).

Thus we can see in contemporary micro-sociology the development of a phenomenon exactly contrary to that which characterized sociology during the period 1880–1930. At that time there was a tendency to replace individual psychology by the study of social groups. Today we see sociology returning to, and in some researchers almost identifying itself with, individual psychology to the degree to which this latter considers man in his relations with his own kind. It is not a question, moreover, of denying any value to the research of the 'science of relations' developed by von Wiese and his students or even to certain sociometric studies. But these are at best *social psychological* studies which consciously eliminate any concrete analysis of human facts as regards *their content and their historical reality* and which, for this very reason, become ideological and distorting from the moment that they are presented as 'sociologies' or as 'sciences of social life'.

Microsociology, moreover, is not the only way to create an a-historical 'sociology'. In France, Gurvitch has developed a 'hyper-empiricist sur-relativist' sociology which recognizes the value of macro-sociology but which abstains from the attempt to establish an *objective and concrete hierarchy* of the groupings indispensable to a real and *concrete* analysis of the structures of social life.[34] He not only rejects historical materialism, but when he mentions the work of Max Weber, contents himself with the laconic remark: 'Much ado about very little.'[35] He lists fifteen criteria, all of equal value, for the classification of groups and three forms of socialization; and he discusses in abstract terms several sociological theories (reproaching them, often, justly, for their unilateral character) without ever relating a single one of them to its historical and social infrastructure.

It goes without saying that in this gloom of 'sur-relativist' abstraction, every concrete content disappears.

To psychologism and relativism may be added the ideological distortions in the *content* of the research. Let us cite a particularly representative case. In an article on methods of studying industrial populations, W. Brepohl, one of the best-known sociologists of the new generation in Germany, after having insisted on the necessity for an objective, unprejudiced (*voraussetzungslos*) study, presents by way of conclusion a plan for such a study, dividing it into four sections: structures (*Gebilde*), norms, forms and values.[32] Section one considers 'the family, the individual, the *gens (die Sippe)*, the business community, the commune, the religious group and the large groupings (country and people).'

In his schema for an 'objective' unprejudiced study of industrial populations, Brepohl has simply 'omitted' the social class.

Thus, psychologistic and microsociological theories,

sur-relativism, ideological distortions and descriptive methods all end by misrepresenting human reality in the same way. They obscure the historical character of this reality and convert the real problems, the problem of the laws of evolution and that of the significance of the individual fact in the *spatio-temporal whole*, into the description of a particular without a context; a particular seen as part of a totality which is implicitly regarded as rigid and susceptible at best only to imperceptible changes. As König says, 'wrench the phenomenon from its historical context' and one no longer studies the 'infinitesimal' from the viewpoint of the philosophy of history but from the viewpoint of its 'adaptation' (to capitalist society, of course). In short, we have here a sociology which no longer seeks to understand but to 'domesticate'.

Needless to say, we are dealing here with repercussions of the fact that the capitalist society of Western Europe has entered into its phase of decline. This phenomenon can be seen more clearly if we consider some evaluations of contemporary sociology by its representatives in the United States, evaluations in which the self-critical element was still possible precisely because American capitalism is still alive – at its apogee in fact – although suffering from the effects of the total situation of world capitalism.

In a volume of essays entitled *Twentieth Century Sociology*, the first article, 'Sociology and the Social Sciences', written by Huntington Cairns, maintains that 'Sociology has been, and is today, a descriptive science. That is to say, it is non-explanatory and its propositions are of equal rank logically, and do not serve as bases for one another. It is a science based directly on detached facts united by a universal hypothesis ... and, as Aristotle observed long ago, might just as well have been otherwise. As hypotheses are introduced into sociology, it will pass over into an explanatory science, and its facts and propositions will become integrated. Until such hypotheses are developed, therefore, the special task of sociology is classification.'[37] In another article in the same volume, Sorokin deals with 'Socio-cultural Dynamics and Evolutionism' and emphasizes the radical difference between the sociology of the nineteenth and that of the twentieth century. The former was dominated by the idea of linear evolution (this is Sorokin's term for the idea of progress); Sorokin finds traces of this 'dogma' everywhere in the human sciences, even in archaeology and prehistory, under the form of the 'standardised stages: Palaeolithic, Neolithic, Copper Age, Bronze Iron and Machine Age.'[38] Fortunately, in the twentieth century, sociology freed itself from the theories of progress, which proved to be 'little productive', and 'researchers directed their attention to other aspects of the socio-cultural transformations, in the first place and principally, to their constant and repeated features: forces, processes, relationships and uniformities.'[39] Reviewing the sociologists who were trying to explicate the essential aspects of social life, Sorokin notes that some of them went in search of '*constant variables* [my italics], such as the density and volume of populations'.[40]

In the same volume, E. Burgess examines methods of research in sociology and the importance of the two fundamental methods, statistical and monographic. The question he asks is: 'What is the importance in the field of sociological research of these two fundamental methods: statistics and monography?' After noting the difficulties encountered in each method, he tells us that some researchers admit 'tacitly or avowedly the insuperable nature of these objections and ... seek out areas where they do not apply'.[41] Some devote themselves to the study of 'human ecology' and 'give little or no attention to the problems of communication and culture'. 'A second reaction' was found in those who present 'a wide range of studies of a descriptive type' with 'concrete materials which are interesting and convincing but where there is no assurance that a second observer would make the same report or arrive at the same conclusions'.[42] Others, finally, have recognized that 'if the personal equation of the research worker was difficult to control in the physical and biological sciences, it was almost impossible to do so in the social sciences'.[43]

Besides the 'nomothetic' method of the ideal types, which he attributes to the sociologists of the classical epoch, that is to 'Simmel, Tönnies, Emile Durkheim, Marcel Mauss, Max Weber and several younger French and American sociologists',[44] Burgess mentions the 'Idiographic' method which studies 'the individual case in all its individuality and completeness',[45] the method introduced into sociology by Thomas and Znaniecki. He notes, however, that 'they did not entirely achieve this goal ... Their conceptual schema was not derived entirely from their data and their data did not in any precise and conclusive sense verify their concepts and hypotheses.'[46]

Finally, after observing that 'there are not, as yet, established statistical methods particularly appropriate to sociological needs,'[47] Burgess cites an American work which is supposed to have succeeded in revealing the main economic, social and political changes in American society from 1900 to 1929, *Recent Social Trends*.[48]

It would be difficult to find better confirmation of our argument. Empirical research (monographs, statistics, interviews) depends on a comprehensive system and only yields answers to the questions posed by the sociologist. It does not even establish the importance of the different factors of social life. The large majority of investigations of this type (as found by us in French and German professional journals, which of course contain reviews of works in English) are conducted in such a way as to preclude the comprehension of the great historical and social processes and, *in the best cases*, direct the interest of the reader to the general problems of inter-individual psychology: social distance, integration, feeling of responsibility, etc. In the majority of contemporary sociological studies, whether theoretical or empirical, the whole of concrete reality, historical and social, tends to disappear completely. As early as 1923, Lukács wrote: 'The monographic method is the best way to obscure the horizon of the problem.'

Bourgeois thought in decline is incompatible with sociological theories which would penetrate to some extent into human reality. Those investigators who perceive the true nature of things, even the conservatives, remain unheard. On the moral plane, social recognition goes to the philosophers of despair; on the scientific plane, to the 'formal' theories, to the investigators of the 'constants' and to 'sur-relativist hyperempiricism'. Behind the scientific intention it is not difficult to perceive renunciation and confessed impotence. This is why it is important to recall once again that, in the field of the human sciences, the desire to understand reality requires, on the part of the investigator, the courage to break with all conscious and implicit prejudices and to recall always that science is made, not from the standpoint of this or that particular group, nor even from an extrinsic and supposedly objective position which presupposes the eternal character of the basic structures of present society, but from the standpoint of freedom and the human community, of man and humanity.

In passing now to the study of Marxist sociology, let us say at the outset that hardly any schematic landmarks exist, since the history of Marxism still requires an enormous labour of documentation and synthesis. It is surprising that this work – at least to our knowledge – has never been done or even attempted in its totality.[49] Such a study could clarify a host of special problems. For example, it seems evident that, in the dispute between Lenin and Rosa Luxemburg, the former reflects, for the most part, the Russian experience, while the latter develops her theories in the light of the German experience. Lenin insists on the importance of the revolutionary party in the revolution, while Rosa Luxemburg is suspicious of it and sees as the essential element the spontaneity of the masses. The difference of opinion comes clear particularly if we recall that, in Russia at the time, there already existed an organized revolutionary party, while in Germany the only socialist party was reformist and that Rosa Luxemburg based her hopes on the creation of certain radical proletarian strata to fight against the leadership of this party. Similarly, it is easier to understand the criticism advanced by Rosa Luxemburg, in 1918, against the agrarian reform in Russia if one remembers that in Germany, an industrialized country, the peasant question was much less important than it was in Russia. Finally, the well-known controversy over the theory of accumulation, in which Rosa Luxemburg maintained that there existed an *economic* limit to the development of capitalism, a limit denied by the Russian theorists, is explained by two considerations:

(*a*) Germany was a country where capitalism had reached its apogee and was approaching this *economic* limit, while in Russia capitalism had hardly begun to develop;

(b) in Russia capitalist development was approaching its *political* limits although those limits were very remote in Germany.

Apart from this specific example, we shall merely stress two facts which seem particularly important to us.

Dialectical thought stresses the total character of social life. It affirms the impossibility of separating its material from its spiritual side. None the less, if one surveys the history of Marxist thought, one always encounters debates between the idealistic, the mechanistic and the orthodox currents. Leaving aside those who, either consciously or unconsciously, break with Marxism (Bernstein, De Man, etc.), it is still true that even within the stream of what can be called orthodoxy there are perpetual oscillations between those currents which stress the acts of men, their chance of transforming the world, and conversely, those which stress social inertia, the resistance of the environment, and the material forces. These oscillations, which are not due to chance, are themselves expressions of social transformations, changes in the conditions of action in the working class movement. All of the great Marxist works which stress the powers of man, his possibilities of changing society and the world through action, are found in the great revolutionary epochs, around the years 1848, 1871, 1905 in Russia, and in 1917. It is enough to mention the philosophical writings of the young Marx (1841–6), his essay on The Civil War in France (1871), *Gosudarstvo i Revolutsia* by Lenin (1917), the *Juniusbroschüre* of Rosa Luxemburg (1916), and *Geschichte und Klassenbewusstsein* by Georg Lukács (1917–22). Conversely, the epochs during which the dominant classes are stable, epochs in which the workers' movement must defend itself against a powerful adversary, which is occasionally threatening and is in every case solidly seated in power, produce naturally a socialist literature which emphasizes the 'material' element of reality, the obstacles to be overcome, and the scant efficacy of human awareness and action. We were surprised to find, when reading the article by Gurvitch on the young Marx (an article which claims to find an opposition, where we find only a difference of accent, between the writings of the young Marx and those of the second part of his life) that the only 'historical' explanation of this difference is, for Gurvitch, the 'polemic with Proudhon' and the 'intellectual environment' characterized by the 'deeper study of classical political economy and the work of Ricardo in particular'. All the same, it seems to us that the hopes aroused by the revolution of 1848, the change of situation resulting from the defeat of the proletarian movement in the course of that revolution, are of distinct importance.[50]

Finally, to bring these remarks to a close, let us note that if one concentrates on the economic aspect of social life and ignores the study of ideologies, this leads to an important error in the evaluation of the theory of finance capitalism and imperialism. On the economic plane the studies of Hilferding and Lenin were remarkable. But the fact that they limited themselves to the study of the economic aspect of reality seems to explain why the thinkers of the workers' movement were led to see European imperialism of the years 1900–15 as the 'last stage of capitalism'. An analysis of the ideological life of that period would probably have allowed for a better grasp of reality and especially the vitality still possessed by Western European capitalism in 1925, 1930 and even in 1939, when its true period of decline began. The transition, on the ideological plane, from Nietzsche and Bergson to Heidegger, Jaspers and Sartre, and the discovery of Kafka and Kierkegaard are symptoms reflective of the evolution of economic and social life, although the significance of those thinkers is incomprehensible except in terms of the latter.

Let us add, finally, that today the development of Marxist philosophy and sociology is limited, at least in Europe, by a complex set of economic and social factors. The concrete aspect which the struggle between the proletariat and the bourgeoisie assumes in our time – the difficulties encountered by the revolutionary movement since 1925–6 (the period in which capitalist regimes surmounted the crisis of 1917–18), the importance which the military problem took on in the U.S.S.R., along with that of the relations of the U.S.S.R. with the capitalist countries, the influence of the U.S.S.R. on the ideological life of the European workers' movements – all of this has produced in the proletariat a spirit of rigid discipline which is extremely unfavourable to research and the intellectual life. That is why, except for the great classical works of Marxism which appeared prior to 1920, the number of studies and really important new investigations has been limited and represents the work of unregimented investigators or thinkers who, like Lukács and Varga, frequently ended by renouncing their own work.

This crisis in the social sciences which exists on both sides of the barricade, although in a different way, creates a situation as paradoxical as it is regrettable. To us it seems that this situation is adequately illustrated by the fact that, among other things, a social phenomenon as important as Fascism has not yet been seriously analysed either by Marxist or by non-dialectical sociologists, and this in spite of the twelve years of National Socialist rule in Germany, in spite of the war, and in spite of the presence of the problem in our own time.

We hope that the preceding observations have illuminated sufficiently the differences between the method of the physical and chemical sciences and that of the social and human sciences. We add only that, seen from the viewpoint of the *more general* relations between theory and action, these two spheres of scientific research become potentially reconcilable : for if the physico-chemical sciences can operate free of all particular value-judgments, it is because the unanimity concerning the necessity of increasing the powers of man over nature has been realized. Since the agreement about value-judgments on this level is a reality, the unity between thought and action is also real and is no longer a matter that need be explicitly discussed. It is clear to everyone that the physico-chemical and natural sciences, however disinterested, serve to dominate and to transform the world.

In the social sciences, on the other hand, the interest of important social groups in maintaining the existing order and in impeding any social change affects the very nature of historical and sociological thought. In calling for a social science free of all prejudice, in affirming, consciously and openly, the historical and transitory character of the present social order, in expressing the hope of subordinating social life to the conscience and action of man, of providing him with intellectual instruments for realizing universal human values, we are simply attempting to realize in this area a relation between the thinker and the whole of social life, a relation both immune to extraneous influences and as objective as that which exists already in the field of the natural sciences, and which can be designated only by a single phrase: the unity of thought and action.

To ask whether the social sciences ought to be dialectical or not means purely and simply to ask if they ought to understand reality or to distort and obscure it: in spite of its different and, *apparently even contrary*, aspect, it is the same battle which, in the seventeenth century, the physicists fought against the particular interests of forces bound to the past and to the Church, the struggle against particular ideologies for a free, objective and human knowledge.

III

THE MAJOR LAWS OF
STRUCTURE

*Economic Determinism; Historical Function of Social
Classes; Potential Consciousness*

The understanding of historical and social life is a
recognition *(prise de conscience)* of the subject of
action, the human community. Scientistic distortion
does not begin only when one attempts to apply to
the study of this community methods borrowed from
the physico-chemical sciences; it is already present in
the mere consideration of this community as an *object*
of study. The other consequences of scientism follow
more or less necessarily from this fundamental
epistemological error.

This does not mean, however, that it is necessary to
renounce all objectivity in the domain of the social
sciences. For there exists not only a *true science*, but
also a *true* or *false* consciousness, and the effort to
realize, on the level of sociology and history, the
adequatio rei[1] and *intellectus* requires as much critical
acumen and rigour as do the physico-chemical
sciences. Different only are the conditions in which
this rigour and critical acumen exert themselves,
above all in the fact that there cannot be at once both
true and *partial* consciousness and that the predominance of the category of totality is the carrier of the
scientific principle in the understanding of social life.[2]
The second precept of the Cartesian method – 'to divide each of the difficulties ... into as many parts as possible, and as might be required for an easier solution'

– valid up to a certain point in mathematics and the physico-chemical sciences, is virtually useless in the human sciences. Here the progress of knowledge proceeds, not *from the simple to the complex*, but from the abstract to the concrete through a continual oscillation between the whole and its parts.

Having already considered the fundamental conditions of historical thought, the problem of ideological distortions and that of the unity between thought and the other aspects of human activity, we will attempt now to sketch in general and schematic lines three major structural elements of social life : the specific importance of economic life, the predominant historical function of social classes, and the notion of potential consciousness.

i

It seems that there have been Marxists who have asserted the 'sole', 'exclusive' importance of economic factors, or at least material ones, for the totality of social life. To tell the truth, we have never encountered any of them, but we ought to add also that we are far from having read Marxist literature in its entirety. Of those authors we know who have stressed economic and social factors, the more important ones – H. Pirenne and Max Weber, for example – were often either unacquainted with Marxism or hostile towards it. Certain 'mechanistic' Marxists like Lafargue and N. Bukharin undoubtedly underestimated the importance of intellectual factors, but they are rather rare, and since the appearance of their works, reactions from the Marxist camp itself have not been wanting.[3] On the other hand, we know of a large number of works which combat an *imaginary* Marxism, urging against it always the importance of ideological factors that no serious thinker has ever denied.

This situation is as understandable as it is paradoxical, and we may be allowed to turn directly to the subject itself and not continue a sterile polemic.

Can we say that in the life of man economic factors enjoy, not a 'unique' or 'decisive' importance, but some kind of privileged position? Strictly speaking, NO; but in fact and in history as it has unfolded until our own day, YES; and that precisely because the individual human being, as well as society, are total facts in which preferred strata may not be singled out. Man is a living and conscious being placed in a world filled with realities that are economic, social, political, intellectual, religious and the like. He sustains the whole effect of this world and reacts upon it in turn. This is what we call a dialectical relation. And precisely because there is not in the consciousness of the individual – save in very rare exceptions – any airtight compartments exempt from the influences of the rest of his personality, he will always constitute a *more or less* coherent unity.[4] That suffices to explain and confirm the prerogative of the effect of economic factors in history past and present; for men are so constituted that in order to love, think or have faith, they must subsist, support and clothe themselves. These areas of human activity undoubtedly *may* have very little effect on thought and the other activities, but *on condition that the satisfaction of the needs to which those activities correspond be largely assured and men devote to them a relatively small portion of their total activity*. Now whether one rejoices in it or not, that still has never been the case for the majority of mankind. The multitude, the oppressed classes and the members of primitive societies have always lived in need, obliged to accord to labour the

87

greatest portion of their time and – in the modern world – they are prey to insecurity and constant fear of the future. Undoubtedly some individual exceptions do exist, but they are extremely rare and, unless the conception of miracle is introduced into historical explanation, it is clearly necessary to admit that, for the overwhelming majority of the human species, economic activity has *always* been of *capital* importance as regards their way of thinking and feeling.

The dominant classes remain. Now they too have always devoted a great part of their time and activity to organizing their economic life and to defending their privileges. On the other hand, it goes without saying that the absence of economic needs creates a style of life which, save in exceptional cases, will act powerfully on the morality and thinking of those who find themselves in this situation (especially in a world where the absence of economic needs is a privilege and, thanks to the misery of the masses, where wealth confers an effectual power on men).

To take an example, one need only think of the court nobility during the reign of Louis XIV. This class did not participate in production; its revenues came in part from lands and feudal privileges, in part from payments for more or less fictitious functions, gifts from the king and royal pensions. Its manner of thinking naturally was influenced by this style of life in which consumption predominated and work did not exist so to speak. In general the court nobility was epicurean or sometimes mystically oriented. That is to say that its moral life, oriented towards, or disgusted by, pleasures, was naturally organized with respect to these pleasures, and not, for example, with respect to work or duty. On the other hand, in whatever had to do with the relations between the sexes, the morality of the nobility (which is expressed, among other ways, in the comedies of Molière) was a great deal freer and more advanced than the morality of the other classes in which man's economic activity, his exclusive inclination to acquire money and material means, established his supremacy and privileges.

At court, where neither men nor women worked, where in order to procure royal favour or the favour of the great, and the social and economic advantages that such favour entailed, the woman was often more effectual and more important than the man. Thus a situation was created of which it is easy to imagine the effect on the manner of conceiving and judging conjugal and extra-conjugal life.

Is that historical materialism? One might object that it is precisely the absence of economic activity on the part of the nobility which is in our description the decisive factor in explaining its style of thinking. In so far as it is directed against historical materialism, however, the objection seems ill-founded to us. For the term 'economic' should be taken in its broadest sense, as a *way of obtaining* income by work, force, exploitation, the enjoyment of certain privileges, etc. In any case, the structure of our analysis conforms to Marx's well-known assertion that 'social existence determines consciousness.' This is a statement in which we think it is necessary to give to the words 'social existence' their broadest meaning, on condition, of course, that this meaning is not made vague, and its exact structure is always preserved in conformity with the historical reality of place and time.

As for ideological factors proper, in the strictest sense of the word, no one would seriously deny their importance. In the case just mentioned, it is probable that the *economic* interests of the French nobility would have required its being oriented toward participation in economic life such as happened in England. All Richelieu's efforts in this direction were in vain, however, and conflicted with the prejudices of a class that believed it degrading to have a hand in commerce and industry. But that these prejudices were able to remain so alive and vigorous, we believe is to be explained in turn by the long and tenacious secular struggle in France between the Third Estate and the nobility, and also by a royal policy which, from the seventeenth century onwards, assured great economic possibilities for existence to a nobility grown more and more decorative and parasitic.

Another well-known example is that of the transition from the ancient to the feudal world. Despite the enormous complexity of a process which extends over several centuries, the sociologist, nevertheless, is led to distinguish two primordial transformations:

(*a*) the transition of agricultural workers from the status of slaves to the status of tenant-farmers (*coloni*), and

(*b*) the transformation of tenant-farmers into serfs.

The first is due primarily to the enfeeblement of Roman military power which exhausted its cheap slave source, the well-spring of the slave economy. This fact obliged Roman landowners, who were no longer able to buy adult slaves at a sufficiently low price on the market, to free those that they already owned, i.e. to give them certain rights, and especially their own earnings, while keeping them attached to the land. In great measure the background of this limited 'liberation' was the need to give the slaves the possibility to start a family, to have and to raise children in order to compensate for market scarcity. Thus was the slave transformed into a tenant-farmer. The Church could sanction and favour this movement but, by itself, the Church would have been able to assure it no more success than it was able to do in the Southern States before the Civil War.[5]

A tenant-farmer is still not a serf, however. The difference between the two resides especially in the existence of a central executive and judiciary power to which the landowner is still obliged to submit. What caused the disappearance of the central power? Evidently it was the decline of a money economy and the return to a natural economy. A state which, in default of money, must call upon its functionaries to pay themselves on the spot will not be able to prevent them from militarizing themselves (they must be armed in order to compel the peasants to pay rents and perform forced labour), nor from becoming independent of the central power (the latter, in default of money, no longer being able to maintain its own army), nor from concentrating in their hands the executive and judiciary power and making their offices hereditary. But what were the determining factors of the transition from a partially monetary economy to a natural economy in the eighth century? If Pirenne is right, particular importance must be granted to the Arab conquest of North Africa and to the refusal of the conqueror to tolerate an exchange of products between Muslim and Christian in the Mediterranean. Here then we are back to ideological factors, if this hypothesis is justified. (At least it is plausible, and that allows it to be taken as the basis for a methodological analysis.) It is highly probable, however, that a more exhaustive inquiry into the reasons and causes of this radical hostility between Arab and Christian (which is supposed to have abated after the Crusades) will uncover in turn economic and social factors which created and sustained this hostility over a long period of time. Those who are familiar with the main materialist analyses will recognize in all this a well-known schema.[6] Undoubtedly we will find personal nuances in each historian, but dialectical materialism as such has never yet denied the influence of ideological factors. It has simply combated every effort to separate them from the rest of concrete social life and to attribute to these factors an *autonomous* and *immanent* evolution with respect to what are customarily called infrastructures.

This leads us to two problems that we must touch on very briefly once more: (1) that of 'influences', and (2) that of 'the relative autonomy' of the different intellectual domains.

(1) It is worthwhile saying here, once and for all, *that influences of any sort explain little, if anything, in intellectual history*, and that because of the existence of two obvious realities: *choice and distortions*. Let us be specific.

At any given historical moment every writer, thinker and, likewise, every social group, is surrounded by a large number of ideas and positions that are religious, moral, political, etc., and these constitute so many *possible influences*. From among them the writer, thinker, or social group selects only one system, or a small number of them, and this selection will *really* be influential. The problem posed to the historian and sociologist then is not that of knowing whether Kant was influenced by Hume, Pascal by Montaigne and Descartes, the Third Estate of France before the Revolution by English political thinkers, but *why they sustained precisely this influence in this particular period of their history or their life*.

In addition, the activity of the individual and social subject makes itself felt, not only in *the choice* of a conception in which the subject rediscovers himself or itself, but also in the transformations which the subject causes the conception to undergo. When we speak of the influence of Aristotle on Thomism, that of Hume on Kant or that of Montaigne on Pascal, it is almost never a question of the real and historical Aristotle, Hume or Montaigne, and of what they actually wrote, saw and thought. Rather it is a question of the thought of Aristotle, Hume and Montaigne as read and understood by St Thomas, Kant and Pascal – which is a completely different thing. We ourselves have analysed a case of this kind by showing the profound modification that Kant's thinking underwent at the hands of the Neo-Kantians (and against which Kant defended himself in advance in his declaration against Fichte who claimed to follow Kant). Neither Fichte nor the Neo-Kantians ever understood this declaration however clear it was, a fact which gave vogue among them to the tenacious legend that Kant wrote it without ever having read Fichtean writings.[7]

Hence it is in the economic, social and psychological structure *of the group which undergoes the influence* that the influence's principal causes must be sought, so that it is still for materialist analyses to explain the influences, and not for the influences to replace, in the explanation, the effect of economic and social factors. As examples, let us take two important instances of the effect of ancient culture on Western thought: the penetration of Aristotelian thought into Europe in the thirteenth century and the rise of Renaissance humanism.

The profound transformation of Christian philosophy in the thirteenth century, the transition from Augustinism to Thomism, is usually explained by the translation and penetration into Europe of Aristotle's writings and the influence that they exercised on the minds of Christian thinkers. This explanation seems inadequate to us because it tells us neither:

(a) why these writings were translated precisely in this period, nor

(b) why they so rapidly assumed such importance in Christian philosophy, despite some initial resistance.

The matter is considerably clarified, however, if we refer to the profound social transformation that Europe underwent at the end of the twelfth century and the beginning of the thirteenth. Its principal traits were the development of towns, the extension of a relatively curtailed area of monetary economy, and the development of monarchical power. Augustinism was a philosophy perfectly suited to a natural economy in which there was neither a central power, nor a radical separation between the temporal and spiritual powers. The growth of towns and the strengthening of the central power rendered this philosophy altogether inadequate to objective reality and created the need for a conception which would give a *limited* but *real* place to the temporal power, to worldly life, and implicity, to reason. It was the rise of royalty that created the conditions for the triumph of the philosophy of Alexander's teacher over the aristocratic philosophy of Augustinian Platonism.[8] (By a flight of fancy it could be said that Augustinism was the philosophy of Canossa just as Thomism opened the way to Anagni.)

Likewise Renaissance humanism, the enormous importance that Greek culture assumed for Western European thought, is explained by the fact that a bourgeois society, no longer oriented towards the beyond, but towards man and the world, broke with the old feudal society and found in the writings of Greco-Latin antiquity a culture and art which were themselves oriented towards the world and especially towards man.

It was their own aspirations and their own mentality that the humanists rediscovered in the writings of Plato and Cicero, and they spoke Greek and Latin until the development of bourgeois society would permit them to say the same thing in their national languages. Moreover, if antiquity continued for so long to have an existential significance for Germany (one need only think of Goethe, Hegel, Hölderlin, Nietzsche), it is precisely because the weakness of the bourgeoisie, the feeble development of capitalism and the absence of a bourgeois revolution did not allow German thinkers to abandon antiquity in order to speak their own language, as did the ideologues of the Third Estate in France and England. At the end of the nineteenth century, ancient culture everywhere became a body of scholarly and academic learning, in Germany as elsewhere.

(2) In speaking of the relations between ideologies and infrastructures, we have no right to pass over in silence the relative autonomy of ideologies.

It is obvious that once certain fundamental elements of a vision are defined on the respective planes of law, religion and art, for example, the jurists, theologians, painters and artists of the period will tend to develop them more and more in all their consequences and to express them in coherent wholes. Hence there is undoubtedly an influence of jurists on law and of theologians on religious thinking, and it would be absurd to want to relate *all the details* of a legal system to infrastructures or other ideological domains.[9] No doubt such a relation does exist for the *content of the fundamental norms* – i.e. for the notion of private property in capitalist society, for the peculiar forms of co-ownership of the land between serf and lord in feudal society. But once these rules become effective, it is the judges, legislators and jurists who, in great measure, are going to determine the forms of their concrete application in the thousand real or possible cases anticipated by the texts and common usage. It is clear that the historian in his work must make the distinction between these two orders of factors, a distinction which must be carried through with respect to the concrete case and does not admit of any general rule. It is unnecessary to say that what is true of law is also true of art, religion, philosophy and all other aspects of the spiritual life. Let us add, finally, that among the coherent expressions in the different domains, expressions which correspond to certain states of relative equilibrium, usually there are transitional forms as well. For the understanding of these it is necessary to consider the immanent need for coherence of the old ideology as well as the counter-effect of the social forces which destroy the framework of this coherence in order to organize progressively the elements of the new vision.

Let us hope that this analysis, the schematic character of which we are better aware of than any-one, will at least have the value of throwing into relief the inadequacy of purely external and empirical history as well as of formal and abstract sociology, and, morever, of illuminating the urgent need for synthesis between individual facts and explicative sociology, a synthesis which alone can bring us nearer a real comprehension of the human facts.

ii

Since we had no intention of presenting here a general account of historical materialism, we will not stress the analysis of its well-known procedure of study (which has never been for anyone either a

dogma or a universal law, but simply the schematization of the most frequently recurring structure). This
procedure concerns the reciprocal effect of the various
domains of social life : means of production, relations
of production, political and spiritual life and development of the productive forces. The reader will find a
copious discussion of these matters in all the classical
works and in the manuals on historical materialism.
Instead, we will dwell on two points which seem
particularly important to us : the *notion of social
classes* and that of *potential consciousness*.

In general the Durkheimians have avoided the
problem of classes in their research. Halbwachs, the
only one among them who dealt with it, limited himself to certain problems concerning the consciousness
of the peasant class and especially the working class,
and by the very virtue of his exceptional penetration,
demonstrated the limitations inherent in the Durkheimian method.

The first two chapters of his work (which are by far
the most important) pose the problem of class consciousness and clearly show that this consciousness is
linked to the role of the members of a class in the process of production.[10] Halbwachs also presents quite
an impelling analysis of alienation and even of the
idea of potential consciousness. Unfortunately, after
this remarkable theoretical introduction, Halbwachs,
as a Durkheimian, seeks *external* and *positive* manifestations of class consciousness and, above all,
manifestations which are nearly universal (thus
abandoning the notion of potential consciousness that
he had glimpsed, however imperfectly). This leads him
to approach the study of social classes from the side
of consumption, undoubtedly an important side, but
one which is nevertheless wholly external; and this
makes of his study an interesting work, but one which

is far from grasping the essential aspects of the problem of social classes.

In a remarkable, although somewhat oblique and cautious article, H. Mougin exposes the errors in every attempt to study classes by concentrating on the categories of consumption.[11] This approach never allows for an identification of the specific features of the various classes which make up a society and, still less, their interests, their structures and their mutual relations. For the relatively clear delineation of a limited number of classes, it substitutes the infinitesimal transitions of the numerous standards of living which exist between poverty and affluence. It might be noted as well that between consumption by workers in a small town and that by workers in a large industrial centre there may be more pronounced differences than between consumption by workers and minor clerks in the same town, especially when it is a question of the major categories of consumption (food, lodging, clothing, etc.).

None the less, Halbwach's work was one of the most serious efforts made by academic sociology to deal with the problem of social classes, and it must be admitted that, in the first two chapters especially, Halbwachs achieved the maximum of understanding that his method allowed him. As for contemporary sociology, we see it divided between the threefold tendency to drown the distinction between social classes and the study of their mutual relations in a mass of countless distinctions and oppositions between other social groups, to deny the historic role of classes,[12] and to define a social class by purely external characteristics which prevent any understanding of the phenomenon.

In speaking of 'types of groupings' Gurvitch nowhere finds any prerogative, special characteristic or particular importance to attribute to classes.[13] He barely mentions in passing that 'the division of society into classes and the struggle of these classes with their repercussions, ideological, psychological, cultural, political, etc., became for *Marx and the Marxists* [our italics] a key to the universal explanation of mass social life and of all historical events.'[14] Gurvitch himself is much more subtle than that. He writes: 'Present-day mass societies are composed of an almost infinite plurality of particular groupings: families, communes, municipalities, departments, locales, public services, states, sects, congregations, religious orders, monasteries, parishes, churches, trade unions and employers' associations with their federations and confederations, co-operatives for consumers, sellers and producers, tourism information and local improvement bureaux, social insurance funds, social classes, occupations, producers, consumers, self employed, political parties, scholarly societies, charitable organizations, athletic and touring teams, and so on to infinity ... All these groups intersect and are delimited, are unified in opposition, are organized and remain unorganized, sometimes from massive blocs and sometimes are dispersed. The course of social life from a macrosociological point of view is no less complex than from a microsociological point of view and remains characterized by an insuperable pluralism.'[15]

As for the 'general schema of classification' of groups, Gurvitch proposes one based on 'fifteen criteria of discrimination the majority of which intersect' and all of which are, in our view, peripheral.[16]

It is no longer any wonder if, in proceeding from such positions or analogous ones, the majority of contemporary non-Marxist sociologists define social classes by features which obscure rather than clarify

99

their social and historical function. By way of illustration, let us mention the definitions of Sorokin and Gurvitch.

For Sorokin, classes are groups which have the following characteristics. '(1) They are legally open to all but are, in fact, semi-exclusive. (2) They are founded on solidarities. (3) They are "normative". (4) They are in opposition to certain other groups (social classes) having the same general nature "X". (5) They are partially organized but mainly quasi-organized. (6) They are partially conscious and partially unconscious of their own unity and existence. (7) They are the characteristic groups of Western society of the eighteenth, nineteenth and twentieth centuries. (8) They constitute multifunctional groups joined by two unifunctional connections: profession and situation. Both of these are to be taken in their broadest sense, and they are joined by a connection based on social stratification and division, i.e. by the existence of a collection of rights and duties essentially opposed to the sharply dissimilar rights and duties of certain other groups – social classes – having the same general nature "X".'[17]

Gurvitch thinks that this analysis by Sorokin is 'one of the most thorough' of those which recently have been made to clarify the 'concept of social class'. Nevertheless he finds that, while 'constituting a step forward', it is too intellectualistic to grasp class as a 'total social phenomenon'. And he proposes another, based not on eight criteria, but on eleven. 'The social class for us is a grouping which is: (1) suprafunctional, (2) large in number, (3) permanent, (4) exclusive, (5) actual, (6) open, (7) unorganized, but structured (except in its embryonic phase), (8) divided, (9) normally refractory to mass penetration (save when it is in power), (10) socially incompatible with

other classes, (11) disposing only of conditional constraint with regard to its members.'[18]

It is clear that Sorokin's intellectualism, as well as
the sur-relativism of Gurvitch, end in minimizing the
role of classes in social life and in history.

Yet a comparison of the two definitions is illuminating. In increasing the number of Sorokin's criteria
from eight to eleven,[19] Gurvitch simply omits the only
two truly important criteria which are to be found in
Sorokin's definition, although they are expressed in
an inexact way and are buried among the others
in numbers 6 and 8. They are the general situation in
production (Sorokin wrongly wrote profession) and
class consciousness (real or potential, a distinction
which is lacking in Sorokin).

Halbwachs, Sorokin, Gurvitch – the further we advance in time, the more ideology pervades the definition and obscures reality beforehand. For Halbwachs,
function in production and consciousness were still
the major components in the understanding of a social
class. In Sorokin they are blended with other characteristics which are peripheral or even non-existent
(such as characteristic 7). In Gurvitch they are
entirely omitted and replaced by eleven peripheral
features. A commentary on this progression is unnecessary.

As partisans of historical materialism, we see the
existence of social classes and the structure of their
relations (struggle, equilibrium, collaboration according to country and historical period) as the key
phenomena for the understanding of social reality
past and present. And we see them in this way, not
for dogmatic reasons of faith or because of precon-
ceived ideas but, quite simply, because our own research, as well as the studies with which we have
been able to acquaint ourselves, have almost always

shown us the outstanding importance of this social group in comparison with all others.

Now if the definition of social classes is an extremely difficult and complex problem, nevertheless it is obvious that such a definition is of interest only to the extent that it may contribute to *explaining to us this importance*, which must have its ground in the very structure of social life. This requirement is satisfied neither by the definitions cited nor by the majority of other definitions that are found in contemporary sociology.

Materialist studies have shown that, in order to define social class, two factors must be taken into account in every case, factors which are mutually dependent *without being strictly identical*: function in production and social relations with other classes. Without purporting to settle the long discussion connected with this problem and, even less, to give an exhaustive definition, we shall merely emphasize here a third element, one which also depends in great part on the other two. But the mere mention of it, we think, will cast special light on the importance of classes in the life of society. It is a factor which has been discovered empirically in the course of our own research on the sociology of knowledge.

From the end of antiquity, up until our own time *social classes have constituted the infrastructure of world-views.*[20]

Let us specify by anticipating a bit the subsequent developments of this chapter. This means that:

(*a*) *Every time it was a question of finding the infrastructure of a philosophy, a literary or artistic current, ultimately we have been forced to consider, not a generation, nation or church, not a profession or any other social grouping, but a social class and its relations to society.*

(b) The maximum of potential consciousness of a social class always constitutes a psychologically coherent world-view which may be expressed on the plane of religion, philosophy, literature or art.[21]

Doubtless all this may be mere coincidence as long as it is not explained and substantiated empirically as a universal truth. We are still far from that. But let us observe that classes are the only groups of which the scales of value are *specific because they aspire, each one, to a different ideal* of harmonious social *organization* in such a way that even collaborations between classes can only be provisory and temporary means to the attainment of essentially different ends. For example, classes may collaborate temporarily on the political level in order to combat a common enemy; yet each aims at a different ideal of man and of social organization.

By way of a *hypothesis* let us add that perhaps the distinction between *ideologies* and *world-views* might be based precisely on the *partial* – and for that very reason – distorting character of the former, and the *total* character of the latter. At least for medieval and modern society that would allow us to link *world-views* to *social classes* so long as they still possess an ideal bearing on the totality of the human community; and to link *ideologies* to *all other social* groups, and to social classes *in decline*, when they no longer act except to defend, without much faith or confidence, privileges and acquired positions.

As for the empirical confirmation of our thesis, it is clearly a question of concrete research which goes beyond the bounds of this small volume. But since Sorokin asserts that social classes are characteristic of European society only since the eighteenth century, let us mention the schematic results of certain studies by Bénichou and of our own works on the intellectual life of seventeenth-century France.

First of all, it seems to us that, if the seventeenth century represents at once the apogee of monarchical power and one of the summits of literary and philosophical creativity in France, the two facts are to be explained by the real equilibrium between the social classes. This equilibrium, on the one hand, afforded a very great freedom of movement to the royal power and on the other hand, led to the abandonment, as unrealistic, of preoccupations with the immediate transformation of society, thus favouring a purely theoretical and literary expression of the world-views of the various social classes. It is because practical preoccupations were remote, because society represented a real equilibrium of the different social classes which, while opposing each other, had, for the moment, each its exact place in society, that world-views were more than ever 'views' (in French: *visions*, following world-views: *vision du monde*) in the proper sense of the word. Because the objective urgency for action was not yet felt, these views could be expressed with such precision on the levels of thought and imagination.

Let us try to show schematically the connections between the various classes, the world-views which correspond to them and their principal expressions in philosophy and literature. The French monarchy developed over the centuries through an actual (although not always free and voluntary) collaboration between the Third Estate and the royalty which struggled together against the feudal nobility. Schematically it may be said that in this collaboration the Third Estate provided the king with money which would allow him to maintain an army and combat the nobility. Among other things, this situation made the sale of offices a marvellous selective criterion for the recruitment of functionaries. Only those who had money wanted and were able to purchase offices: enriched commoners, loyal to the king and hostile to the nobility by virtue of class interest. But as we shall soon see, this harmony between the monarchy and its functionaries of common origin – the *gens de robe* – disappeared when the alliance between the monarchy and the Third Estate came to an end under Louis XIV.

From Montaigne to Pascal the evolution of the *noblesse de robe* was important. And *La Logique* of Port-Royal reproached Montaigne for having 'feared' that the duties of a representative to parliament 'might reduce him somewhat'. For, 'having taken care, very needlessly, to inform us in two passages of his *Essays* that he had a page whose office was a very useless one in the house of a gentleman worth 6,000 *livres* of rent, he did not show the same concern to tell us that he had also had a clerk who had been representative to the parliament of Bordeaux.' 'Apparently, however, he would not have concealed this fact from us if he had been able to find some Marshal of France who had been a representative of Bordeaux'.[22]

During the childhood of Louis XIV an event took place which marks a turning point in the history of France: the Fronde. For a brief moment this uprising could appear dangerous because it resulted from the momentary conjunction of the extreme forces of the past: the revolt of the princes and the first stirring of the great revolutionary force of the future – the Third Estate. To these two factors must be added the agitation of Parlement, of the *gens de robe* who acted under the illusion of being able to lead the uprising and play the role of arbiter between the people and the princes. The danger was not real, however, because the coalition was too incongruous. Precisely on account of these oppositions, the monarchy soon proved to be the decisive factor in the balance and, as such, more powerful than ever. Nevertheless, the position of the monarchy changed, and with it, its policy. It was no longer the ally of one class against another, but – for a short time – was an external force which placed itself outside and beyond classes. This was expressed, among other ways, in an external event: the changing of the royal residence. The king of the Third Estate was nowhere more secure than in his good town of Paris. But the Fronde gave him to understand that an effective alliance had come to an end. The Sun King went to live at Versailles, equidistant from the towns of the commoners and the estates of the nobility. Also it must be said, once and for all, that the creation of the court of Versailles, with its pomp and etiquette, was not a mere cultural event, and even less, a caprice of Louis XIV; it was first of all a political measure of genius analogous to that of the sale of offices. The latter had made possible the formation of a staff of functionaries originally of the Third Estate; the changing of the royal residence allowed for the maintenance of the noblemen far from their lands where they could again become sources of opposition. And, by means of substantial financial advantages, this measure enabled the king to bind them to his person and to the interests of the monarchy, thus hastening the transformation of the *noblesse d'épée* into a *noblesse de cour*.

Thus we see in France under Louis XIV at least five classes, *all of which find expression on the planes of philosophy and literature*: namely the great lords, the *noblesse de cour, the gens de robe*, the well-to-do Third Estate, and the common people composed of artisans and peasants.

The great lords, the dukes, who resented this transformation more keenly than the rest of the nobility, could never be content to accommodate themselves to the bourgeois society which was in the process of constituting itself, precisely because the real power that their ancestors possessed, and that they lost, was greater. The new social world taking shape before them appeared as an egoistic world of shabby ambition. This proximity of the concrete reality that was encroaching upon them, this negation symmetrical to the affirmation of the eighteenth-century philosophers, who themselves were too close to a social reality which they combated with a demand for immediate change – this prevented the great lords of the seventeenth century, as it prevented the writers of the Third Estate in the eighteenth century, from expressing themselves through the creation of a conceptual or imaginary world. Reality was too close and, for the lords, simultaneously too deficient and too powerful, for them to grasp it beyond the immediate datum, event or psychology. This is the social background of the *Memoirs* of the duc de Saint-Simon and the *Maxims* of the duc de la Rochefoucauld.

We have already characterized the situation of the *noblesse de cour* : a life of continual pleasure, a sexual code freer than that of any other class, equality of man and woman, and acceptance of monarchical society in which each class had its place, on condition that the nobility might keep its own, which it considered predominant. The epicureanism of this class expressed itself on the philosophical level in the works of Gassendi; the totality of its vision, on the literary level, in the works of Molière.[23] Let us mention the main ones. *L'Avare* is a satire of the bourgeois as such whose principal defect, in the view of the *noblesse de cour*, was the amassing of money, and the making of money into an end in itself instead of spending it.

Tartuffe is a satire of the curate who, with his Christian claims, interferes in the lives of the laymen and who, for the courtiers, could only be a dangerous and selfish hypocrite. *Le Misanthrope* is Jansenism seen from the courtiers' point of view. The austerity, the claim to absoluteness, of the Jansenists, their retreat into 'the desert' of Port-Royal des Champs, were perhaps lofty and grandiose but, in any case, excessive and devoid of good sense, i.e. of understanding of real life and its demands. *Don Juan*, the fourth comedy of character, is a satire of some madcaps who elevate atheism and epicureanism into an explicit and aggressive system at court. In this play, moreover, one feels that Molière's attitude towards his hero is essentially different from the one he had towards Harpagon, Tartuffe and even Alceste. (For example, see the scene in which Don Juan saves the life of Don Carlos and becomes known to Elvira's brothers who are searching for him to avenge their honour.) In the same way it can be seen how easily Molière's other plays can be inserted into this perspective: *Amphitryon, L'École des femmes, L'École des maris, Le bourgeois gentilhomme, Georges Dandin*, etc.

Let us further add that this analysis casts a certain light on the social infrastructure of French casuistry in the seventeenth century. It is not very likely that the Jesuits themselves were a debauched lot. Why then did they adopt the casuistry, so un-Christian, that Pascal flagellated in *Les Provinciales*? Are we going too far in supposing that this was the only way for them to maintain their influence on the court nobility? In the face of the impossibility of transforming their lives and mentality, the result of their state of existence, it was only possible to adapt the letter of Christian precepts to the spirit and style of life of the court nobility if one wanted to keep the latter's allegiance.

Beside the court nobility the profile of another class appears: the *gens de robe*, the majority of whom were ennobled. We will call them the *noblesse de robe*. Commoners by origin, fulfilling effective social functions as against the *noblesse de cour*, they regarded the latter with a disdain mixed with envy on account of its pomp and privileged social situation. The *noblesse de robe*, living not only in Paris, but chiefly in the provinces, involved with commoners by virtue of their daily lives and affairs, and often related to them, were indisputably enticed by the rationalistic individualism of the bourgeoisie. (Some of them became renowned mathematicians.) But, on the other hand, since their function was the most considerable component of their success, they were too bound to the monarchy to be able to accept rationalism in all its consequences. Hence, it is this class in France in which developed the tragic vision wherein man appears torn between two contradictory claims that the world prevents him from reconciling. This is the central idea of Pascal's *Pensées* and of Racine's tragedies. Man is both great and weak. Great by virtue of his consciousness, his demand for totality and absoluteness; weak by virtue of the inadequacy of his powers to realize this demand. A 'reed', but 'a thinking reed'. The only greatness possible for man is the rejection of compromise and, implicitly, the rejection of the world and the acceptance of the wager on the existence of a God and an eternity which are not at all certain. Thus takes shape the *Deus absconditus*, the hidden God to whom Pascal appeals in the face of the inadequacy of men, of Port-Royal itself. 'Port-Royal is afraid ... *ad tuum Domine Jesu tribunal appello*.'

It is unnecessary to add that the religious institution

which expressed the extreme consequences of this ideology was Port-Royal, the tenacious persecution of which is explained, among other ways, by the extreme susceptibility of the monarchy confronted by an ideology which threatened to influence its functionaries and detach them from it.

The Third Estate, the ascendant class, engaged in the process of winning more and more real power, and radically opposed to the nobility, was naturally optimistic, individualistic and especially rationalistic. The individual, his reason, his will, his glory, constituted its supreme values. Its mentality is expressed in the works of Descartes and Corneille; the religious institution which corresponds to it, *in part*, is the Oratory. (We say in part only, because, in the Oratory, there was a mystic current – Bérulle, Condren, etc. – which was aristocratic by nature and constituted the natural counterpart in religious terms of the epicureanism of the court nobility.)

Finally, the lower classes speak through La Fontaine's *Fables*, too numerous to be enumerated here, but each of which was written from the point of view of the common people : the peasants, the ass, the lamb, the rat, the horses, etc. In the *Fables* of La Fontaine, man is no longer the thinking reed, but 'the reed which bends and does not break' in the fable *'Le chêne et le roseau'*.

This schema, which we will develop more fully elsewhere, but which already seems very promising in its general outline, shows the primordial importance of social classes for the understanding of the literary and spiritual life in France in the seventeenth century. Obviously it is for concrete research to show its validity in detail and also to perceive in what measure other analogous explanations might be valid for different periods and countries.

To conclude this theme let us add only one remark. We believe that a social class is defined by: (a) its function in production; (b) its relations with the members of other classes; and (c) its potential consciousness which is a world-view.

In concrete research, however, there are always one or two of these factors which are more easily perceptible and easier to grasp at first. For example, in the case just analysed it would have been difficult to decide, on the basis of infrastructual factors alone, if the *noblesse de robe* did or did not constitute a social class. The existence of a specific conception, which found its most radical expression in Jansenism and especially in Pascal's *Pensées* and in Racine's plays, led us to decide definitely in favour of an affirmative answer. However, it is the absence of such a specific conception in the sixteenth century which would have made us hesitate in viewing the *gens de robe* as a social class at this earlier time.

Inversely, if we have said that the *Fables* of La Fontaine expresses the vision of the common people, peasants and artisans, the analysis of the infrastructure shows that there are at least two different classes within this mass: peasants and urban artisans who are still undifferentiated on the ideological level. (Since Hegel, Marx and Piaget we know that for individuals, as for groups, the grasping of an event by consciousness comes usually only after the event.)

Here, as everywhere else, there is no general and universal rule for research if it is not that of adapting oneself always to the concrete reality of the object studied.

iii

Now we come to the most important, but also the most delicate problem in our study: the problem of *potential consciousness*.

The partisans of positivist and descriptive methods – in the best of cases, when they are not dealing solely with institutions and external behaviour – recognize consciousness only as a *real consciousness* which exists *now*. Once they make the concession of acknowledging a non-physical reality, they demand, at the very least, that it possess the principal qualities of the material world. Thus it is a *different*, but analogous domain that they decide to add to the physico-chemical sciences. It seems to us, however, that this concession does not suffice and that it is necessary to admit a *qualitative* difference between the two realms of human knowledge. If man is not a machine, but a *living* and *conscious* creature; if the existence of three *qualitatively* different kinds of being must be acknowledged in the universe – the inert, the living and the conscious – there must also be qualitative differences between the respective methods of the physico-chemical, biological and human sciences. It goes without saying that a *qualitative* difference does not imply a *metaphysical* difference and that it neither excludes the emergence of one of these realities from the other nor the existence of transitional forms.

Leaving aside for the moment the problems of method in biology and even in psychology, we hold that the fundamental concept in the historical and social sciences is that of *potential consciousness* which we shall attempt to analyse on the basis of the works of Max Weber and the Marxists.

In the Durkheimian literature we have encountered

this concept only once – scarcely touched upon – in the book by Halbwachs, *Les classes ouvrières et les niveaux de vie*. Speaking of the consciousness that the working class has of its unity, Halbwachs conceives that this consciousness might not be a reality, but rather a possibility. Yet it is difficult to determine if he clearly distinguishes this possibility from a physical potentiality.

By contrast, this concept has a fundamental significance in the sociology of Max Weber, although he sometimes confuses ideas which we think must be distinguished and, above all, clarified. First, there is the 'ideal type'. Weber was well aware that human reality could be comprehended only on the basis of what he called 'ideal' constructions which, although not real, are closely related to reality none the less. For Weber, capitalism, *homo oeconomicus*, and Protestantism are 'ideal types'. Linked to the ideal type, moreover, seems to be the 'objective possibility', which envisages the consequences that a fact would have had whether an event occurred or not (contrary to objective reality). For example, one might imagine the historical evolution that would have taken place had the Greeks lost the Persian Wars. Yet it is necessary to introduce into one of these two categories a hypothetical commander-in-chief who would have known all of the objective data of a battle (which in fact he did not know).[24] We do not believe that Weber offers a precise and explicit distinction between ideal type, objective possibility and maximum of potential consciousness.

As for the selection and structure of these concepts, Weber seems to have been content with a psychological criterion. The scientist conceives them arbitrarily and it is their fruitfulness in research which enables the good ones to be distinguished from the bad. But for certain 'ideal types' (the rational types), he provided us with a deeper analysis. Some ideal types like *homo oeconomicus*, capitalism, and Protestantism are constructed by imagining men who act in an *entirely* rational way in the choice of their means. Because of their rationality, we are able to *understand* them completely, and these ideal types aid us in understanding the concrete reality which is more complex and confusing. At the opposite pole there is the completely irrational man, the madman of whom an ideal type can no longer be constructed because he can no longer be *understood*, but merely *explained*.

As a result of these analyses it seems necessary to us : (a) to distinguish three methodological instruments which are related perhaps in certain respects, but are none the less different; and (b) to pose the problem of the conditions of their validity, a problem no longer pragmatic but epistemological.

In Weber's canon of analyses, we distinguish at least *three* scientifically different instruments : (a) static schematizations; (b) historical schematizations and the distinction which follows there from between determinants and contingent factors as regards the event under study; and (c) the notion of potential consciousness.

First let us examine the schematizations. They concern reality and, as such, they *are common to all areas of scientific thought*. At most three types must be distinguished : *formal* and *axiomatic* schematizations – geometry, logic, mathematics; *real* schematizations realized daily in every physical or chemical experiment; and *mental* schematizations proper to the empirical, non-experimental sciences – history, sociology, economics, etc. They all have the same goal : to study a reality disengaged from contingent factors in which only the elements judged essential are operative, all other factors being eliminated, either rendered or supposed constant. The geometrical square eliminates the inaccuracies of the empirical square, logical schematization the inaccuracies of real thought. The physicist in the laboratory renders artificially constant all factors outside of those whose variation he wants to study. The sociologist speaks of 'feudalism' or 'capitalism' by abstracting the heterogeneous factors which always exist in concrete reality. These schematizations are good or bad according to whether they extricate the essential factors in the constitution of the reality under study or whether, on the contrary, they remain attached to subordinate factors. The latter often leads to a grave error, that of bringing together heterogeneous and even antithetical phenomena and thus obscuring the true structure of reality instead of clarifying it.

Moreover, if Weber is right (we still have no definitive opinion on this point), and if every good schematization in the human sciences implies behaviour which is *partially* rational (a rationality not of goals, but at least of techniques), this would prove, contrary to certain contemporary philosophies, that rational behaviour is one of the constitutive factors of human nature.

To end this analysis we would like to give an example of good and bad schematization in the human sciences. In a more or less conscious manner, the point of departure in classical political economy is the most general schematization, that of *homo oeconomicus*, the man who pursues always and everywhere his economic interests in a rational way. Marx has shown that this most general schematization, which the economists studied above all from the standpoint of the individual, implies, when translated into a coherent economic order, the existence of a form of production for the market and the elimination of transitional difficulties from one branch of production to another, as well as the elimination of differences in wealth. This then will be called a *simple merchandise-producing society*. If we introduce a new factor into this schematization, the differentiation between workers, having only their labour to sell, and capitalists, owning the means of production, we obtain the less general economic schematization of *capitalist society*. (Marx studied this schematization in detail in *Capital* simply by adding to it, in volume III, the differences in the technical development of the different branches of production.) And if to this schematization of capitalist society we add a new factor to bring us yet closer to concrete reality, a large number of possibilities then present themselves to us. We would like to analyse here two of them which are most often used. Into the general schema of capitalist society composed of capitalists and workers a distinction may be introduced between the owners of the means of production and those who use them (what are usually called incorrectly capitalists and entrepreneurs) and the division of the entire income of the capitalist class into interest and profit. Or, indeed, a third class, working with its own means of production (middle classes, peasants and artisans), may be added to the two classes constituting capitalist society.

Now although each of these two developments in schematization takes its point of departure from concrete reality, they still do not possess the same scientific value. The distinction between capitalists and entrepreneurs has no decisive economic importance. Whether, on an average, the respective share of these two groups in the surplus-value be half or as against that, one quarter and three-quarters, this will not necessarily have any *decisive and qualitative* consequences for the operation of the economy. Moreover, the distinction is of the same order economically as the distinction between landowners, industrialists, merchants, etc., a division created by the distribution of the surplus-value among the different groups of capitalists. But if the distinction between 'capitalists' and 'entrepreneurs' has only a limited scientific significance, it possesses, on the other hand, great ideological import. For it tends to mask the opposition between workers and capitalists in order to replace it by a factitious opposition which would bring together workers and 'entrepreneurs' and oppose them to owners of property and capital. (It is unnecessary to say that these latter may sometimes be petty landowners or petty shareholders.) By contrast, the inclusion of owners, working with their own means of production, reconciles this schema with concrete reality and possesses *considerable* scientific significance, because it allows us to understand better the economic and social evolution of capitalist society in its totality.

Hence one is a good schema, the other a bad one, and that for a definite reason, namely that one obscures, whereas the other makes manifest the real division of capitalist society into social classes and the mutual relations between them.

At the root of the distinction between good and bad schemata, as at the root of any scientific conception, there is thus one criterion of truth : the adequacy of the conception to objective reality.

This holds true to the same degree for the dynamic schematization of historical evolution and for the distinction between factors which have a causal value and factors which are accidental and contingent.

As regards these schematizations which are common to all sciences, it is necessary to single out *the notion of potential consciousness*, which to us seems to be the principal instrument of scientific thinking

in the human sciences. We will leave aside its ontological bases in the nature of man considered as a being
who transforms the world and society. We will also
leave aside its use in individual psychology.

In sociology, knowledge is found *on the double
plane of the knowing subject and the object studied,*
for even external actions are the actions of *conscious*
beings who more or less freely choose and judge their
mode of conduct. The physicist has to take into account only two levels of knowledge, the ideal norm –
the applicability of the conception to things – and the
actual learning of his time, the value of which depends upon its distance from the former. Now if the
physicist must take into consideration only these two
levels of knowledge, the historian, and especially the
sociologist, must take into account at least one inter-
mediary factor between them, *the maximum of potential consciousness* of the classes which constitute
the society under analysis.

Real consciousness is the result of the multiple obstacles and deviations that the different factors of
empirical reality put into opposition and submit for
realization by this *potential consciousness.* However,
just as it is essential for the understanding of social
reality not to submerge and confound the activity of
the essential social group, the class, in the infinite
variety and multiplicity of actions of other social
groupings, and also of cosmic factors, so too it is essential to separate the *potential consciousness of a
class* from its real consciousness at a certain moment
in history. Real consciousness is the result of the
limitations and deviations that the actions of other
social groups and natural and cosmic factors cause
class consciousness to undergo.

Man is defined by his possibilities, by his tendency
to enter into community with other men and to

establish an equilibrium with nature. Authentic community and universal truth express these possibilities *over an extremely long historical period*. 'Class-for-itself' (as opposed to class-in-itself) and the maximum of potential consciousness express possibilities on the level of thought and action *within a given social structure*. Some examples will serve to illustrate the capital importance of this notion in the different areas of social life and social research.

In social and political action it is evident that alliances between social classes can only be made on the basis of a minimum programme *which corresponds to the maximum of potential consciousness of the least advanced class*. In 1917, when Lenin, to the horror of the majority of Western socialists, sanctioned the distribution of land to the peasants, which seemed contrary to every socialist programme, he simply recognized the fact that the Russian proletariat, in order to win the Revolution, needed the alliance of the poor peasants and agricultural day-workers, and that *agricultural collectivization exceeded the grasp of the potential consciousness* of the peasantry in a non-socialist society. In the same way, the nationalism of the proletariat of colonial peoples and the temporary abandonment of its specific claims condition its collaboration with the bourgeoisie in these countries in their struggle for independence. During the French Revolution, the demand for *legal* equality represented the maximum of potential consciousness for the bourgeoisie. Comprehension of the fact that legal equality is purely formal and does not guarantee any economic equality surpassed the potential consciousness of the revolutionary bourgeoisie.

In passing to the sphere of scientific thought, we will mention one well-known example, that of Quesnay's *Tableau économique* (1758) which remained absolutely incomprehensible to bourgeois economists up to the First World War. This was no accident.

The Physiocrats have always been troublesome for historians of economic doctrine. Partisans of a natural order, free trade and a great many other, apparently bourgeois, ideas and claims, the Physiocrats always supported two ideas which seemed to them as obvious as they appeared absurd, and even contradictory, to subsequent economists: (a) the exclusive productivity of agriculture and the sterility of commerce and industry; and (b) the necessity of having only landowners pay taxes.

In reality their doctrine becomes perfectly coherent and comprehensible if one puts oneself in the position, not only of the Third Estate, but also in the position of the royalty menaced by it. Influenced by the thinkers of the Third Estate, and realizing at the same time the danger of revolution, the inadequacy of a policy of repression, and, above all, the fact that royal power depended up an equilibrium between the classes, Quesnay, a thinker of genius, recognized that the only chance of saving the monarchy was to reinforce the nobility in order to create a counterpoise to the Third Estate. A sophisticated economist, he declared that industry and commerce produced only workers' salaries and capitalists' profits, whereas agriculture produced ground rent as well, which could constitute the economic basis for a strengthened aristocracy. Whence the *perfectly coherent* programme of removing capital from commerce and industry and orienting it toward the capitalization of agriculture and, at the same time, of freeing the menacing Third Estate from all taxes, burdening only the nobility with them, the landowners who were supposed to reap all the advantages of this increase provided by the ground rent.

This investigation into the possibility of harmonizing the economic interests of the different social classes in order to avert a revolution and strengthen the monarchy led Quesnay not only to create the science of economics, but also to formulate directly the *ingenious schematization of economic relations between the social classes* that he called the *Tableau économique*.[25] The Physiocrats were perfectly aware of the importance of this discovery. Louis XV, it seems, saw fit to print it with his own hand. Mirabeau called it one of the three discoveries, *viz.*, 'writing, money and the *Tableau économique* ... which have given to the political sciences their principal strength'. Never the less, when the founder of liberal economy, Adam Smith, who was Quesnay's direct disciple, published the *Wealth of Nations*, there was no longer the least trace of the *Tableau*. The problem of harmonious economic relations between social classes lay beyond the *potential consciousness* of the liberal bourgeoisie. In fact, the *Tableau* has always been ignored by the main representatives of liberal economics until recent years. Even in 1910, G. Weulersse wrote a book on the Physiocratic movement, 1,380 pages in large octavo, in which he devoted only ten pages to the *Tableau* without perceiving its importance at all. And the most authoritative manual on the history of economic doctrines at the beginning of the century (by Gide and Rist) informs us that the *Tableau économique* aroused in contemporaries an incredible admiration which only raises a smile today.[26] M. Gide's account of it 'gives only an imperfect idea of the criss-crossing and repercussions of revenues, whose rebounds the Physiocrats amused themselves in watching with childish pleasure. And they fancied they saw in them reality itself. The fact that they could always trace the exact account of their billions intoxicated them.'

By that time, however, the *Tableau* had long since re-entered economic theory. Karl Marx was the first of nineteenth-century social theorists to recognize its importance. Speaking of the *Tableau* in several places in *Theorien über den Mehrwert (Theories of Surplus Value)*, he wrote that 'never had political economy known such an ingenious idea', for 'Smith was simply a successor of the Physiocrats; he catalogued and specified in a more rigorous manner the different articles of the inventory without succeeding in giving to the whole the exactness of development and interpretation of the *Tableau économique*, despite Quesnay's erroneous hypotheses'. And Marx devoted the greater part of the second book of *Capital* to Quesnay, introducing, however, one important modification. He replaced the primary classes of Quesnay's time, landowners and sterile classes, nobility and Third Estate, with the essential classes of his own age, workers and capitalists.

The subsequent destiny of the *Tableau*, called *Modes of Production* in Marxist literature, is also interesting. Marx, who, like Quesnay, wrote in the prospect of revolution, understood immediately the importance of Quesnay's ingenious idea. But by the time the second book of *Capital* appeared, capitalism had become stabilized; there was no revolution in the offing at all. And in the Marxist camp no one – excepting Engels, of course – understood the importance of the *Modes*. One Marxist critic even asked why Engels published calculations so devoid of interest. The first who understood their importance was Tugan-Baranowsky in Russia, eleven years before the revolution of 1905. And he understood them from the point of view of the bourgeois Russian Revolution as an affirmation of the possibility of an indefinite development of capitalism. This was the interpretation in turn that the reformist Marxism of Western Europe gave them with

Hilferding, Kautsky, etc., and also, on the *economic plane*, the interpretation that Russian Marxism gave them with Lenin, Bukharin, etc., who recognized only *political* limitations to the development of capitalism.[27] It was only in 1913, on the eve of the First World War, that Rosa Luxemburg thought it possible to discern in them an economic limitation on capitalism. Since then, in Marxist literature the discussion has lengthened into hundreds and thousands of pages and, to the extent to which the problem of the Revolution is posed to the contemporary bourgeoisie, representative thinkers like Schumpeter and Keynes have also returned (although in an obscure and confused manner) to the problems posed by Quesnay's *Tableau économique*.[28]

Whether the *Tableau* is childish or a work of genius, it is possible to see the extent to which the *social conditions* and *potential consciousness* of the respective classes acted on the way this lengthy yet simple text, which presents no particular difficulties, was read and interpreted.

Finally, to close this subject, let us cite some examples in the history of social and philosophical thought. We have said already that, in the work of Saint-Simon, there are, among many other errors, two relatively important ones. (a) He never saw the possibility of a real conflict between the proletariat and the bourgeoisie, and (b) he believed in the possibility of a lasting alliance between the Bourbons and the Third Estate (industrialists, in his terms). We think it is very important that the historian should not regard these two errors as existing on the same plane. The first is the result of the limits of the *potential consciousness* of the Third Estate at the beginning of the nineteenth century; the second has causes of another kind and could have been avoided by a bourgeois thinker of the same period.

As regards philosophy properly speaking, we have attempted to show elsewhere at what point the impossibility of understanding the unity of thought and action, of being and the norm, followed from the limits of the *potential consciousness* of the German bourgeoisie at a certain period of its history. For the same reasons, Voltaire could not comprehend Pascal, the Neo-Kantians, Kant, etc. In the next chapter we will return to the importance of the notion of the maximum of potential consciousness in the history of philosophy and literature.

EXPRESSION AND FORM

On the question of understanding the objective meaning of historical events, and especially of philosophical, literary or artistic works, several positions
stand out in the literature of the nineteenth and
twentieth centuries. Using the terminology of E. Lask,
we may divide these positions into two large groups:
those of analytic logic (empiricism, rationalism) and
those of emanative logic (Romantic or Hegelian history, Spengler's works, etc.).

For analytic logic, the only *objective reality* is the
isolated fact that empiricism accepts as such, whereas
rationalist history passes judgment in the light of the
universal values of reason. But, in the one case as in
the other, one remains on the plane of the external
behaviour of one or more individual things, whether
it concerns the study of a battle, the economic activity
of a group, or the study of a literary or artistic current or work. It is on the basis of these discretely
given concrete facts that the historian is subsequently
able to construct sequences and even to establish laws
or causal explanations. Accordingly, in order to remain within the analytic logic advanced by the
Heidelberg Neo-Kantians, and to avoid all emanation-
ism, Max Weber had recourse to his ideal type of
rational behaviour which allowed him to *understand*
human actions, but without adding anything to their
external aspect. No one will deny the important ser-
vice of analytic history which, by its worship of concrete facts, has contributed most to elucidating the

facts known and used today by history and the social sciences.

It is also true that the partisans of emanative history always reproach analytic history for treating human facts like physical facts, for proceeding from their external appearance and being content with establishing between them more or less factitious relations, which ultimately are analogous to the descriptions and laws of the physicist.

By contrast, the emanative conception of history implies two ideas that we intend to examine separately. The first is the conviction that the majority of human manifestations can *be comprehended* only as expressions of a deeper reality that the emanationists usually conceive as a supra-individual reality (spirit of the people – Volksgeist – in the Romantics; objective spirit in Hegel; various 'souls', such as the Classical, Arab and Faustian, in Spengler).

We recognize the important contribution that this way of envisaging history has brought to the understanding of numerous historical events, and especially to the understanding of the cultural manifestations of social life, religion, law, art, philosophy, etc. It is also true, however, that the partisans of analytic history always reproach emanative historians, not only for a certain dilettantism, in which they are undoubtedly often right, but also and especially for the speculative and metaphysical character of the majority of their supra-individual entities (spirit of the people, objective spirit, soul of a civilization, etc.).

Fortified by its positive contribution to historical understanding and by the justified criticism which it formulates against the opposite position, each of these two attitudes thus appears to us inadequate to serve as a general foundation for the human sciences. Is there a possibility of synthesizing them? We think dialectical materialism offers such a possibility because, while denying the existence of every metaphysical and speculative entity, it none the less considers spiritual life as the *expression* of a deeper and broader human reality. How is such a synthesis possible?

For dialectical materialism there is no supraindividual consciousness. Collective consciousness, class consciousness, for example, *is only the totality of states of individual consciousness and of their tendencies resulting from the mutual influence of men upon each other and their effects on nature.*

But here we arrive at the second central idea of the emanative conception, an idea that dialectical materialism *wholly* accepts and for the sake of which it opposes all analytical thinking in a radical way. Dialectical materialism does not believe that the totality of individual states of consciousness is an arithmetical sum of autonomous and independent unities. On the contrary : with Pascal, Kant, Hegel and Marx it holds that each component can only be comprehended in terms of the totality of its relations with the other components, i.e. with the whole through the effect that each component exercises on this whole and the influences that each sustains from it.

Now we have already said that in society, at least since antiquity, the nature of this totality of relations between individuals and the rest of social reality is such as to give rise to the continual formation of a certain psychic structure which is common to a very great extent to the individuals who form one and the same social class. It is a psychic structure which tends toward a certain coherent perspective, a certain maximum of awareness of self and of the universe, but which also implies more or less rigorous limits in the awareness and understanding of itself, the social

127

world and the universe. In inclusive and statistical terms this means that social classes form the infra-structures of world-views and tend to express them coherently in the various spheres of life and the spirit.

Here we see superiority of historical materialism: it can study intellectual and artistic phenomena, not from without, but in terms of their contents as expressions of a *collective consciousness*, without being obliged thereby to recur to *metaphysical* and *speculative* hypotheses such as the spirit of a people or the soul of a civilization.

Every manifestation is the work of its individual author and expresses his thought and his way of feeling, but these ways of thinking and feeling are not independent entities with respect to the actions and behaviour of other men. They exist and may be understood only in terms of their inter-subjective relations which give them their whole tenor and richness. Pascal had already perceived this when he wrote: 'The parts of the world all have such a relation and such a connection with each other that I believe it is impossible to know the one without the other and without the whole ... I consider it equally impossible to know the parts without knowing the whole, and to know the whole without knowing the parts.' And Kant believed he was breaking new ground in 'establishing two new principles of great importance for metaphysical knowledge', the first of which is that 'no change can be produced in substances except to the extent that they are mutually connected. The mutual dependence of substances determines then the mutual alteration of their condition.'

If we speak of the *expression of a collective consciousness*, however, one misunderstanding must be avoided. A work is not yet this kind of expression by the mere fact that it may be understood solely on the basis of the relations of its author with the whole of social life. This holds good for every component of the human world and even of the physical universe; for the most original work as for the most eccentric one; ultimately even for that of a madman. *A mode of behaviour or a text becomes an expression of collective consciousness only to the extent that the structure which it expresses is not peculiar to its author but is shared by the various members who form the social group.*

What we would like to emphasize now is the importance of a concept which Lukács utilized in 1905 and 1917, but which he seems to have abandoned today: the concept of 'Form'. If every feeling, every thought and, ultimately, every mode of human behaviour is *Expression*, it is necessary to distinguish within the totality of expressions the particular and preferred group of *Forms* which constitute the *coherent* and *adequate* expressions of a *world-view* on the planes of *behaviour*, *concept* and *imagination*. Hence there are forms in life, in thought and in art, and their study constitutes one of the important tasks of the general historian, and the most important task of the historian of philosophy, literature and art and, above all, of the sociologist of knowledge.

World-views are social facts. Great philosophical and artistic works represent the *coherent* and adequate expressions of these world-views. As such, they are *at once individual and social* expressions, their content being determined by the *maximum of potential consciousness* of the group, of the social class in general, and their form being determined by the content for which the writer or thinker finds an adequate expression.[1]

To conclude this subject, let us add two observations the importance of which will certainly not escape the reader, although we cannot develop them here.

(1) Sociology of knowledge may study world-views on two different planes, that of the *real* consciousness of the group, as researchers such as Weber and Groethuysen have studied them, for example, or that of their *coherent*, exceptional expression in great works of philosophy and art, or even in the lives of certain exceptional individuals. (The latter plane corresponds more or less to the maximum of *potential* consciousness.) The two planes *complement* and mutually support each other. Though it may not seem so at first, it must be said that the second plane is often easier to study than the first, precisely because world-views are expressed there with more clarity and more preciseness; whereas a study of the development of a new world-view in the *real* consciousness of a group offers a much more difficult task, on account of the multiple forms of transition and the enormous complexity of entanglements and mutual influences which constitute social life.

On the other hand, it is obvious that the study of great philosophical and literary works requires an exhaustive job of analysis since, ultimately, one must attempt to distinguish, not only the content, but also the external *form* of the work *on the basis of its total scope (vision d'ensemble)*. It is a task which, up to now, has rarely been attempted, but one which seems to us to constitute one of the chief tasks of literary criticism and the analysis of styles. To give but one example, let us take representative statements of two major seventeenth-century philosophies.[2] It is obvious that the equilibrium and perfect balance of the two terms of *Cogito, ergo sum*, or of the two terms of 'I think, therefore I am', express wonderfully well the optimism and equilibrium of Cartesian philosophy;

whereas the vertical ascendancy of the first element and the abrupt fall of the conclusion in '*Le silence éternel des espaces infinis m'effraie*' ('The eternal silence of infinite space frightens me') concentrates and expresses the very essence of the tragic vision. Likewise, paradox, as a stylistic means, is almost inevitable in a great philosophical writer with a tragic vision who proceeds from the fundamental idea that man is at once both *great* and *humble*, i.e. that one and the same subject can be defined only by two apparently contradictory propositions.

(2) In addition, it is obvious that the number of possible world-views is much smaller than the number of situations in which we find them and also smaller than the number of social classes encountered in the course of history. Almost every one of the great visions known to us turned out to express economic and social situations which were different and, in several cases, even contradictory. One need only think of the aristocratic Platonism of Greece and also, with several differences, that of medieval Augustinism which subsequently became in Galileo and Descartes one of the chief means of expression of the Third Estate in opposition to the aristocracy. Likewise, the tragic vision which is encountered again in Kant and Pascal expresses, in the former, the ideology of one of the most radical elements of the eighteenth-century German bourgeoisie and, in the latter, that of the *noblesse de robe* in seventeenth-century France. This explains, among other things, these renaissances of the tragic vision, but at the same time it raises the most difficult problem of every sociology of knowledge, that of a *typology of world-views*. These world-views are obviously limited in number, but it would be difficult to say whether they all have found expression already

in the intellectual and artistic history of the periods known to us.

Nevertheless, we can forsee that this typology, which we are still far from having achieved,[3] will require more or less complex analyses since, henceforward, the need becomes clear to distinguish several different levels. Individualism, for example, constitutes a common basis on which positions as different as stoicism, epicureanism and scepticism became differentiated in the course of time.[4] And on yet a higher level, it is necessary to distinguish the ancient stoicism, with its pessimistic cast, from the stoicism of the sixteenth and seventeenth centuries which is optimistic and full of confidence.

Be that as it may, this typology, which would be a major step in the development of intellectual history and sociology of knowledge, appears to us at the moment still far from being realized, or even realizable, because it calls for long preliminary concrete studies. It is important not to lose sight of either in the course of doing partial research.[5]

APPENDIX

At the beginning of this study, we noted that human 'facts' never speak for themselves but yield their meanings only when the questions put to them are inspired by a philosophical theory of the whole. To illustrate this point we will outline here, in a completely summary manner, an example of a complex of relationships holding between the writings of Pascal and Racine on the one side and the religious, social and political events of their time on the other, a correlation which we discovered during a philosophical historical inquiry in which we are now engaged.[1] The discovery of this correlation was totally unforseen by us because our theoretical position did not require it at all, much less one so precise and strict. The case with which we are concerned is privileged and exceptional since the correlation of the social life to its expression in the works of writers and philosophers is generally much more complex and more mediatized. The study of Pascal's thought led us in fact to distinguish between at least two periods in his writings: the first characterized by the separation of regions of knowledge which are amenable respectively to sensory experience, reason and authority; the second, which we call tragic, characterized, *among other ways*, by the affirmation of the *truth of contraries*, the inadequacy of *all* human knowledge, the *primacy of ethics*, and the *wager*.

Now, the transition from the first of these positions to the second occurs at all events after the composition of the last of *Les Provinciales*, hence between

March 1657 and August 1662, the date of Pascal's death.[2]

However, it is in March 1657 that the Bull of Alexander VII, which expressly condemns the *Augustinus*, makes its appearance in France. It is also in March 1657 that this Bull is received by the Assembly of the Clergy, which reiterates its demand for the signing of the Formulary of Submission. These events rendered the persecution (of the Jansenists) imminent and destroyed all hope among the Port-Royal religious and solitaries of appeal to any earthly power. Placed, as the fragment of the XIXth *Provinciale* puts it, 'between God and the Pope', there remained to them only the 'appeal to God' – i.e. tragedy.

Although we had perceived from the beginning of our investigation the correlation between these events and the development of the thought of Pascal, we did not assign to it any great significance, since we assumed that the relationship was probably conscious and in any case easily understandable. Its greater significance became evident, however, when the study of Racine showed that his dramatic work, far from being isolated, could be fitted into a complex of analogous relationships which this time were probably, for the most part, subconscious and involuntary. The chronology of Racine's tragedies and other dramas can in fact be established in the following manner.

After having passed his childhood and adolescence in the Jansenist atmosphere of the secondary schools and the college of Beauvais, Racine departed for Uzès in 1661, resolved to commit an act which, from the viewpoint of Jansenist morality and thought, was one of the most reprehensible imaginable. In fact, without the slightest religious vocation, he resolved to obtain an ecclesiastical benefice through the influence of his uncle. It is easy to imagine the indignation of his aunt, a nun at Port-Royal, and very probably also that of his former teachers. Perhaps one even has the right to suppose that, given his inner development, his own conscience was not completely at rest.

It turned out, however, that the desired benefice was slow in materializing and difficult to obtain, and Racine resolved to try his fortune in another field, that of literature, writing, among other works, two plays: *Alexandre* (1665) and *La Thébaïde* (1666), which are not tragedies and reflect nothing of Jansenist morality and thought.

Now, in 1665, at the height of the persecution of the Jansenists, Nicole, in response to Desmarets de Saint-Sorlin, published, first *Les Imaginaires*, and then, *Les Visionnaires*, in which he criticized his opponent for, among other things, having formerly composed theatrical works and of having been a corrupter of public morals. It is quite improbable that Nicole, engaged in a full defensive battle against the persecutors of Port-Royal, intended to create a new enemy by attacking, indirectly, Racine. Whatever his intention, however, Racine, whose conscience could not have been completely tranquil, felt himself under attack and responded with one extremely sarcastic letter, which he published, and with another, which he declined to publish.

Now, in 1667, Racine's *Andromaque*, the first of his tragedies, appeared, followed by *Britannicus* and *Bérénice*, three plays characterized by a radical rejection of the world and of life. Their heroes, Andromachus, Junius, Titus and also Bérénice ultimately (after her 'conversion') incarnate perfectly the morality and world-view of Port-Royal. All three plays are appeals to God. By writing them Racine created a new genre in world literature: pure tragedy, or the tragedy of refusal.

However, *Bérénice* is followed by four plays in which the heroes try to live in the world, and in three of them the world itself begins to assume positive traits. The first, *Bajazet*, performed for the first time in 1672, can be characterized as the perfect *pièce du compromis*.

Then, in 1669, the Peace of the Church provisionally established a compromise, a *modus vivendi*, between the Jansenists and the royal power, which temporarily brought a stop to the persecutions; moreover, the years 1668–70 were characterized by a general policy of internal conciliation, accompanied by the suppression of the Chamber of Justice, a decree favourable to the Protestants, the conversion of Turenne, activity aimed at the reunion of the two churches, etc. This policy seems to have borne fruit, since the social troubles which generally characterized the reign of Louis XIV abated for a few years.

In 1673 Racine produced *Mithridate*, his first genuinely historical play, since in it the national mission of the protagonist, the common struggle against the Romans, renders Mithridates human and resolves the individual problems and conflicts of the play. Then, in 1672, Louis XIV undertook his first great military expedition, the Dutch War, in preparation for which he had probably taken all the measures of internal conciliation of 1669. This war soon became a war against the entire Hapsburg Empire.

In 1674, Racine produced *Iphigénie*, the subject of which is the difficulty encountered and sacrifices required by the war of the Greeks against Troy, a war which the gods bring to a successful conclusion without demanding the sacrifice of Iphigenia. On the periphery of the play, however, the tragic figure reappears in the person of Eriphile.

Now, in the political and social sphere, the war ran

up against a considerable number of unforeseen difficulties due to the obstinate resistance of William of
Orange (who did not hesitate to open the dikes and
flood his own country) and the coalition which soon
formed between the Dutch, Austrians and Spanish. In
1677, Racine returned to tragedy with *Phèdre*, the
theme of which is the same as that of *Mithridate*: the
king is believed to be dead; the king's wife who loves
the son of the king tries to tell him of it, but the report turns out to be false and the king returns. But
this time the world no longer possesses a positive
value; the king's journey is unimportant, the conflicts
are tragic and irresolvable. It might be added that this
tragedy is less specifically Jansenist and closer to
Greek tragedy.

Now, in France itself, the protracted war demanded
greater and greater sacrifices, and general discontent
grew. In 1675 a number of revolts broke out and
soon became the culminating point of the reign, em-
bracing most of western France: Brittany, Le Mans,
Bordeaux.

On May 30th, 1676, Louis XIV effected the first
breach of the Peace of the Church by the decree
against Henri Arnauld, Bishop of Angers, a decree
which raised once more the problem of the Formulary.

We know that from 1677, the date of *Phèdre*, to
1689, Racine produced nothing. In 1689 and again in
1691, however, he produced two plays about the manifest God, plays affirming the victory of good over evil
in this world.

Now, as Charlier and Orcibal have already pointed
out, at the end of 1688, the English Revolution occurred, and the former king, James II, had taken
refuge with his family and his court in Saint Germain-
en-Laye.[3]

Thus we have the following table:

1656

Constitution of Alexander VII confirming the condemnation of the Jansenists, published in France in 1657.

1657–62

Period in which Pascal writes the fragments which will make up *Les Pensées* and which constitute the first coherent expression in world philosophy of the tragic vision.

1657

Adoption of this constitution by the Assembly of the Clergy which reiterates its demand for the signing of the Formulary.

1655–61

Racine lives in the Jansenist environment of the secondary schools and the college of Beauvais and there receives his education.

1662–5

Racine writes *La Thébaïde* and *Alexandre*.

1661–2 or 1663

Racine at Uzès hopes to obtain an ecclesiastical benefice through the influence of his uncle Sconin, the vicar-general. His hopes do not materialize.

1666–70.

Racine writes the three tragedies of refusal to

1665–6

Nicole publishes, against Desmarets de Saint-Sorlin:

compromise life and the world, extreme expressions of Jansenist morality: *Andromaque* (1667), *Britannicus* (1669), and *Bérénice* (1670).

Les Visionnaires. Racine believes that he is under attack and counterattacks with two letters, of which he publishes only the first.

October 23rd, 1668
Conversion of Turenne.

1669
Peace of the Church. Compromise between the Jansenists and the royal power. General policy of conciliation, suppression of the Chamber of Justice, decree favourable to the Protestants. Great efforts to reconcile the churches. Performances of *Tartuffe* are authorized.

1671–2
Racine writes *Bajazet*, the play of compromise.

1672–3
Racine writes *Mithridate*, his first historical play, in which the war against Rome transforms the beast into man and permits the resolution of all individual problems.

1672–3
Beginning of the Dutch War. First great military expedition of Louis XIV. William of Orange opens the dikes and floods the country.

1673–4
Racine writes *Iphigénie*, his second historical play.

1673–4
The war encounters certain unforeseen difficul-

Subject: a war which encounters certain difficulties and calls for great sacrifices. The gods end, however, by becoming reconciled and assure a victory. In the background of the action appears the tragic character, Eriphile.

ties and becomes progressively burdensome. Alliance between the Emperor, Spain, the Duke of Lorraine and the Dutch. Defection of England.

1675–7

Racine writes *Phèdre*. Returns to tragedy. Returns to the theme of *Mithridate*, but from a tragic point of view. History no longer exists. The conflicts are irresolvable. No compromise is possible.

1675

After a period of calm which lasts from 1669 to 1670, popular insurrections break out again in Brittany, Le Mans and Bordeaux. The tensions grow. All Paris is telling the tale, true or false, of a lace worker who killed his children and himself in order to avoid paying taxes. (Letter of Mme de Sévigné, July 31st, 1675.)

1676

May 30th. Anti-Jansenist decree against Henri Arnauld, raising once more the problem of the signing of the Formulary.

1688–9

Esther

Late 1688

English Revolution.

1689–91
Athalie. The plays of the
manifest god and of the
victory of good over evil
in this world.

Whatever the import and meaning of these cor-
relations, which we will study in depth elsewhere,
they seem to us to raise certain problems which cannot be ignored. For the time being, it seems important
to note that the philosophical and literary expression
of the tragedy of refusal, which is one of the most
important developments in the history of Western
culture, emerged in France between 1657 and 1670,
that is, in the thirteen years which coincided closely
with the great persecution of the Jansenists and the
demand for the signing of the Formulary. One might
even extend this generalization to the whole of
seventeenth-century tragedy, since *Phèdre* was written after the decree of May 30th, 1676.

NOTES

PREFACE

1 The most important modification concerns the transition from crisis capitalism to organized capitalism, which we had not foreseen when we were writing this book, in 1951.

2 For there are still, to be sure, some crises whose origins are to be found outside of industrial society, in the movements of decolonization and independence in the underdeveloped countries which have repercussions in western Europe (such as, for example, in the case of the Indo-Chinese and Algerian wars for France).

3 It should be said, however, that the link between sociological thought and organized capitalism is complex and (let it be stressed in order to avoid any misunderstanding) certainly involuntary and not conscious. The more a given theory eliminates, by its very structure and by the methods it elaborates, the problem of meaning and that of history, the less it needs to become explicitly involved in the defence of the existing social order. As formalistic structuralism is completely divorced from social and political problems, its implicit value-judgments arise on the methodological level. Raymond Aron, who retains many of the traits of the liberal rationalism of the Enlightenment, takes a much more explicit position in favour of organized capitalism. At the end of the line are to be found certain former Marxists who, having scarcely assimilated the intellectual methods and structure of contemporary sociological thought, finish by becoming direct and almost crude apologists for technocratic society.

CHAPTER I

1 We believe that history embraces *past*, *present* and *future* facts. But in order to avoid a discussion that would force us to postpone the subject that concerns us at the present time, we ask for the moment only why men are interested in the past. The answer would be valid *a fortiori* for present and future historical facts.

2 Yet it should be added that in certain epochs, in Western Europe, e.g. in the seventeenth and eighteenth centuries, they had another function, that of establishing certain ideological values, whence their great importance for the philosophy of this period.

3 Bruneau et Heulluy, *Grammaire française, Classe de 4-ème.* The authors, however, realize that this statement is not absolutely valid, for they conclude, 'But *nous* can be a true plural.' To which the students might respond, '*We* prefer to take the test Monday evening.' Let us note that the example is not a happy one. Taking a test is not, in the present school system, a communal action of which the subject would be a true community.

CHAPTER II

1 It goes without saying that it concerns a *relative* totality which is only one element of the totality men-nature.

2 The merit of having stressed the radical separation between the given and the normative must go to Lévy-Bruhl: cf. his work, *La morale et la science des mœurs.* In *Les règles de la méthode sociologique,* Durkheim still maintained, in the well-known section on the normal and the 'pathological,' that rules of conduct could be deduced from the simple objective study of the facts. On the whole his students do not seem to have followed him on this point.

3 We write 'perhaps' because it is a question of emphasis.

4 Undoubtedly it will be objected: (a) that for Durkheim this definition of crime is provisional; and (b) that he himself speaks of crimes 'which play a useful role in society' (p. 70) and are a condition of progress. But, on the one hand, neither Marx, nor Engels, nor subsequent Marxists have ever pretended to have exhausted the analysis of primitive communism and, on the other, Durkheim has always insisted on this definition of crime and on the subsuming under the same concept of two forms of behaviour essentially different by nature.

Let us also mention that Durkheim defines the 'normal' forms of social life by the fact 'that they are general within the entire compass of the species and are met with again, if not in all individuals, at least in the majority of them' (p. 55), thus identifying the 'normal' with the real. Likewise he 'provisionally' defines social reality by the criteria of constraint and respect for 'institutions'. 'Institutions ... constrain us and we find our due in their functioning and in this constraint itself' (p. xxi).

All of this reflects the conservative ideology which endorses the existing social order.

5 The situation was not the same in the sixteenth or even the seventeenth centuries.

6 To give an example, more easily understandable by virtue of its temporal distance: in the seventeenth century a partisan of Ptolemaic astronomy could display exceptional ingenuity and acumen in an effort to adapt his hypothesis to the empirical data. He could show exemplary intellectual honesty, admit the deficiencies of his theory in the explication of the facts, reproach other researchers for passing over certain things in silence, contenting themselves with approximations, etc. All this would not make his work more scientific inasmuch as he had failed to renounce at the start the hypothesis of the earth's immobility and refused to enter into conflict with the interests and ideology of the Church.

7 Max Weber's studies on method in the historical and social sciences were drawn up over fifteen years, in the course of which he progressively elaborated and clarified his thought. Together they bulk very large and we will concentrate, for the moment, only on those ideas which particularly interest us.

8 In his last essay – deservedly renowned – on the theory of science, '*Wissenschaft als Beruf*', mentioning in passing his own anti-pacifist position, Weber vehemently attacks those professors who admit value-judgments into their teaching. 'The true teacher will guard against imposing any position whatever from the authority of his chair, either explicitly or by suggestion, the latter naturally being the most treacherous way of allowing the facts to speak' (p. 543). 'I propose to prove, by analysing the works of our historians, that the whole understanding of the facts is halted where the scientific scholar permits the intrusion of his own value-judgments' (p. 544). Let us add that the last name mentioned in this essay as answering to his ideal of the objective scholar appears to us today as a symbol. It is the name of a young aesthetician, hardly known at the time, Georg von Lukács (p. 522).

9 One of the essays in the book, dealing with the transition to socialist society, is entitled 'The Change in the Function

of Historical Materialism'. Cf also K. Marx, *Theses on Feuer-bach.*

10 For G. Gurvitch, see note 18 below. Marcel Mauss, who died in 1949, was the founder of the French School of Social Anthropology and the master of almost every living French anthropologist. The first volume of his Collected Works has just been issued (1968) by Les Editions de Minuit, Paris. (Ed. Note)

11 Maurice Halbwachs and Georges Davy both succeeded Durkheim in the Chair of Sociology at the Sorbonne (created 1932). Davy and Gurvitch were joint professors for a time. The Durkheim, Mauss and Weber works are available in English: Allen & Unwin, 1912; Cohen & West, 1954; and Allen & Unwin, 1930, respectively. (Ed. Note)

12 *Soziale Welt,* a review edited for the Community of Institutes for Social Research in Germany by the Institute for Social Research in Dortmund, I, 3, April 1950, p. 71.

13 The works of Professor T. Geiger, of Aarhus (Denmark), may be cited as an example of descriptive research conducted with a deep sense of historical sociology.

14 René König, *Soziologie Heute,* Regio-Verlag, Zürich, 1949, p. 121.

15 *Soziale Welt,* I, 2, January 1950, pp. 35–51.

16 We shall have occasion to return, in the following chapter, to the notion of *potential* as a fundamental concept of the human sciences (objective potential in Weber, potential consciousness in Marx and Lukács).

17 For Karl Mannheim, who died in 1947, see especially *Essays on the Sociology of Knowledge,* Routledge & Kegan Paul, London, 1952. (Ed. Note)

18 G. Gurvitch, *La vocation actuelle de la sociologie,* Presses Universitaires de France, Paris, 1950, pp. 569–81. (Georges Gurvitch was the most influential French sociologist at the time of writing, being editor of the *Bibliothèque de sociologie contemporaine* and the *Cahiers internationaux de sociologie,* as well as co-editor of *Twentieth Century Sociology,* Philosophical Library, New York, 1945. His *Déterminismes sociaux et liberté humaine,* Presses Universitaires de France, Paris, 1955, as well as later works, should be consulted. [Ed. Note])

19 Pitrim Sorokin, 'Qu'est-ce qu'une classe sociale', *Cahiers internationaux de sociologie,* II, 2, 1947. p. 66. (The principal works of Pitrim A. Sorokin of Harvard University are *Contemporary Sociological Theories,* Harper, New York, 1928, and

Social and Cultural dynamics, 3 vols, American Book Co., New York, 1937 [with a fourth vol. in 1941]. [Ed. Note])

20 In the French translation of Bukharin's work there is a comma in place of the *and*, but the meaning is not changed and the context shows that, in spite of his notorious mechanism, Bukharin never identified the two things.

21 Loc. cit., pp. 70–1.

22 L. Moreno, 'La méthode sociométrique en sociologie', *Cahiers internationaux de sociologie*, II, 1947, pp. 95–6. (For J. L. Moreno's 'sociometry' see, in English, *The Sociometry Reader*, edited by J. L. Moreno, Free Press, Glencoe, Illinois, 1960. [Ed. Note])

23 Let us add, in order to understand the meaning of this phrase, that Gurvitch designates his own position as sociological sur-relativism.

24 G. Gurvitch, loc. cit., p. 602.

25 See L. Goldmann, 'Matérialisme dialectique et histoire de la littérature', in *Recherches dialectiques*, Gallimard, Paris, 1958.

26 On this subject see L. Goldmann, *La communauté humaine et l'univers chez Kant*, Presses Universitaires de France, Paris, 1952.

27 The French language does not even have a word analogous to Cartesian, Hegelian or Spinozist by which to designate the disciples of Pascal. The term *'Pascalisant'* indicates a scholar who studies Pascal without accepting his ideas. However, there is no word for a researcher who studies Descartes without accepting his thought. This is because Descartes expressed the thought of the Third Estate which created modern French society.

28 It is enough to think of the reverberation among German intellectuals of the famous phrase of Burckhardt announcing the 'era of the terrible simplifiers'.

29 H. Cohen, *Kants Begründung der Ethik*, Berlin, 1877 and 1899, p. 313. The 'we' indicates the extent to which he is sure that he speaks in the name of the entire social class.

30 Gabriele Le Bras's main work is *Études de sociologie religieuse*, 2 vols, Presses Universitaires de France, Paris, 1955–6. A selected bibliography of the voluminous work of C. Lévi-Strauss can be found in Cape Editions, no. 1 : C. Lévi-Strauss: *The Scope of Anthropology*, Cape, London, 1967. (Ed. Note)

31 See L. von Wiese, *System der allgemeinen Soziologie*, 2 vols, Munich 1924–9; *Soziologie: Geschichte und Hauptprob-*

leme, Berlin, 1926; *System der Soziologie als Lehre von den sozialen Prozessen und den sozialen Gebilden der Menschen*, Munich, Second ed. 1933. In English, see *Systematic Sociology, etc.*, adapted by H. Becker, Wiley, New York, 1932. (Ed. Note)

32 Let it be understood that we do not wish to deny the importance of all measurement or all quantitative valuation, but only to criticize a certain fetishism of measurement such as that expressed in a sociological study of the 'social scientist' in the United States, in which the authors, in studying the variations in comportment among American sociologists, write, 'We do not here take into account "personal" motivations, such as love of truth or an appetite for knowledge, since there do not exist valid data on this matter and since it is practically impossible to assign to them today even an approximate place on a calibrated scale of national distribution.' (R. Merton and D. Lerner, 'Le "Social Scientist" en Amérique,' in *Les sciences de la politique aux États-Unis*, Colin, Paris, 1951.)

33 L. Moreno, 'Sociométrie et Marxisme', *Cahiers internationaux de sociologie*, VI, 1949, p. 73. In another passage in the same article, Moreno speaks of 'two Marxes: the man of science anticipating sociometry and the politician,' p. 66.

34 It is true that, sometimes, he seems to recognize in principle the necessity of a true hierarchy; thus on page 270 of his work, *La vocation actuelle de la sociologie*, he writes, 'The unity of global society with reference to the multitude of particular groups which contend with each other, delimit each other and mutually hold each other in check, or which unite with each other, mutually penetrate each other or, finally, form into massive complexes, is confirmed by the predominance accorded to the nation over its parts and is expressed in a *variable hierarchy of groupings*, the relative stability of which constitutes the global social structure ... The specific hierarchy of groupings can serve as the most objective criterion for the study of global social types.' But if we look, as he asks us to do, at the work in which he has undertaken the study of this hierarchy, we read at the beginning of the chapter devoted to this problem that 'the infinite complexity, the richness of forms and contents of the whole global society ... make it difficult to establish any sociological types without taking a particular social activity as a landmark ... The classification of the types of global societies will thus yield widely differing results according to whether one looks at it in the light of its effects on economic, re-

ligious, moral or legal phenomena.' (G. Gurvitch, *Élements de sociologie juridique*, Aubier, 1940, p. 120.) And again: 'Since we are aware of the essentially pragmatic character of every classification of the types of total social phenomena, a classification which admits of multiple variables according to the aim pursued, we will limit ourselves to sketching some schematic types of global societies as a function of the study of juridical phenomena' (ibid., p. 211). Given the fact that the 'most objective criterion' varies with the societies studied and above all with the point of view, it does not seem to us particularly apt to disengage the structure from the historical and social reality. Gurvitch, wishing to reconcile a highly systematic *form* with a 'hyperrelativist' *content*, becomes extremely sensitive to the weaknesses of different sociological theories which he criticizes; in the development of his own thought, however, he runs the risk of combining the disadvantages of system (abstraction) with those of relativism (absence of structure), without preserving their respective contingent qualities: a synthetic and structured view and an approximation to the immediate reality.

35 Gurvitch, *La vocation actuelle de la sociologie*, p. 40.

36 W. Brepohl, 'Industrielle Volkskunde', *Soziale Welt*, II, 2, January 1951, p. 123.

37 *Twentieth Century Sociology*, Philosophical Library, New York, 1945, p. 15. The first concrete 'sociological law' mentioned in this volume, on page 24, is formulated thus: 'The number of persons going a given distance is directly proportional to the number of opportunities at that distance, and inversely proportional to the number of intervening obstacles.' The second appears on page 135 and affirms that there is a decline in the marriage rate during times of economic depression.

38 Loc. cit., 103. (The author refers to a French translation, we refer to the original. [Ed. Note])

39 Loc. cit., 107.

40 Loc. cit., 108.

41 Loc cit., 23.

42 Loc. cit., 24.

43 Loc. cit., 24.

44 Loc cit., 30.

45 Loc. cit., 29. (See W. I. Thomas and F. Znaniecki, *The Polish Peasant in Europe and America*, Badger, Boston, 1918, and A. Knopf, New York, 1927. [Ed. Note])

46 Loc. cit., 29.

47 Loc cit., 33.

48 Loc. cit., 34.

49 There are, however, some remarkable studies of Marxist theories of the state in Lenin and of the theories of accumulation in Rosa Luxemburg.

50 G. Gurvitch, *La vocation actuelle de la sociologie*, pp. 600–1. Equally surprising is the statement that: 'Only George Plekhanov, Edward Bernstein and, to some extent, Bukharin ended by accepting this point of view' (the activist humanism of the young Marx, taken up again by Engels). On the one hand Gurvitch omits mention of Lenin, R. Luxemburg and, in philosophy, G. Lukács who, in 1917–18, *without knowledge of* the still unpublished manuscripts of the young Marx, had recovered their content; all this not to mention H. Lefebvre, *Le matérialisme dialectique* (Alcan, Paris, 1939; the translation of a recent edition is to be found as no. 27 of Cape Editions, under the title *Dialectical Materialism*, London, 1968. [Ed. Note]); K. Korsch, *Marxismus und Philosophie* (Leipzig, 1923); and many other much less important works. On the other hand, the work of Bukharin, cited by Gurvitch, has always been considered by Marxists as mechanistic, since it underestimates the importance of consciousness and of human action. In 1925 Lukács wrote of it in a review, 'Bukharin's aim, which was to write a popular manual, should make the critic indulgent towards his conclusions in detail, above all when it is a matter of peripheral areas. This aim, as well as the difficulty of procuring in Russia the works which he needed, excuses, for example, the fact that in speaking of art, literature and philosophy, he refers almost exclusively to second-hand accounts and often does not consider the most recent literature on the subject. The danger which results from this practice is however augmented by the fact that in trying to write a book to be understood, B. *tends to oversimplify the problems themselves* ...' Then, after some criticisms on specific points, Lukács continues, 'But we do not wish to linger over details, for much more important than the absence of depth and these deviations is the fact that B. estranges himself, on certain essential matters, from the real tradition of historical materialism and this without being objectively correct, without even going beyond, let alone reaching, the level of his predecessors. B. begins thus to approximate, in a disquieting manner, bourgeois materialism (contemplative materialism, to use Marx's term). Without even speaking of Marx and Engels, the criticism of this doctrine by Mehring and

Plekhanov, the rigorous distinction between its incapacity to understand history and the specifically historical character of dialectical materialism does not seem to exist for B. In his philosophical considerations, B. tacitly eliminates, without even combating them, all of the elements which, in Marxist method, derive from classical German philosophy ... Bukharin's theory, which resembles very much the bourgeois materialism inspired by the physico-chemical sciences, thus takes on the aspect of a 'science' (in the French sense of the word) and obscures occasionally in its concrete applications to society and to history the essential element of Marxist method: the act of linking all economic and sociological phenomena to social and human relations.' (G. Lukács's review of Bukharin in *Archiv für Geschichte des Sozialismus und der Arbeiterbewegung*, Leipzig, 1925, ii, pp. 217–18.)

<h4 style="text-align:center">CHAPTER III</h4>

1 On condition the word *res* is interpreted not as 'object' or 'thing' but as *reality* in the broadest sense.

2 This, *among other things*, because the *'recognition'* already of itself (and not merely by its 'technical' applications) changes the structure of society.

3 See Lukács's review, already cited, of Bukharin's book. Let us also mention that a long section of Plekhanov's well-known manual, *Fundamental Problems of Marxism*, is devoted to the criticism of two thinkers, the first of whom *overestimated* the importance of economic factors, the second, the importance of the class struggle. These thinkers were Espinas and Eleutheropulos, professors in Paris and Zürich. (For H. Pirenne, see, in English, *Medieval Cities*, Princeton University Press, Princeton, 1925; *Economic and Social History of Medieval Europe*, Kegan Paul, London, 1936, and *A History of Europe from the Invasions to the XVIth Century*, Allen & Unwin, London, 1939. [Ed. Note])

4 Complete coherence is obviously as exceptional as the total absence of coherence. But the existence: (a) of some individuals who win at the national lottery, and (b) of some who play often without *ever* winning does nothing to discredit the validity of the statement that those who play regularly at the national lottery lose a large part of their money.

5 Let us add that, behind the ideological superstructure of

the Civil War, there was also the need of the industrial Northern States to be assured of free manpower and an internal market.

6 We are supposing that the hypotheses are sound; a supposition which has no *logical* importance.

7 Fichte himself affirmed it first in a letter to Jacobi. Rickert took it up again: 'I am taking this occasion to remark that I too entirely approve what Medicus says on the subject of Kant's declaration against *Die Wissenschaftslehre* in August 1799. It is almost certain that Kant never studied Fichte thoroughly. When Kant was seventy-four years old he wrote to Tieftrunk (April 5th, 1798) that he 'knows *Die Wissenschaftslehre* at present only through the review in the *Allgemeine Literaturzeitung*', and no one will concede that he might have read it afterwards. His "declaration", then, possesses no scientific significance at all and, from the human point of view, it is to be regretted that he expressed himself publicly against Fichte precisely during the dispute over atheism. No doubt one may *excuse* that on account of his old age, but if certain Kantians recently have availed themselves again of the authority of Kant against Fichte, relying on this declaration, that must be rejected in the most decisive way.' (H. Rickert, in *Kritizismus*, Kolf Heise, Berlin, 1925, p. 53.) And we ourselves have heard the same view expressed in a course on Kant given by Professor F. Medicus.

8 Let us add that the most radical phase of Aristotelianism, Averroism, seems to have developed precisely in areas where commerce was most highly developed: in Padua, the seat of the University of Venice, and in Flanders. It is certainly no coincidence that the two great representatives of radicalism (Averroist and Pantheist) on the Faculty of Arts in Paris in the thirteenth century were Siger of *Brabant* and David of *Dinant*.

9 Although sometimes such relating might be possible. But it is definitely a special case and not the general rule.

10 The source the author is citing does not appear to be named; it is probably M. Halbwachs, *La classe ouvrière et les niveaux de vie*, Alcan, Paris, 1913. (Ed. Note)

11 See note 10. The source is probably H. Mougin, 'Le problème des classes' in *Annales Sociologiques*, série A, fasc. 4, Presses Universitaires de France, Paris, 1941. (Ed. Note)

12 We have already mentioned the typical example of Brepohl's article.

13 Among the fifteen criteria adopted by Gurvitch for the

classification of groupings, it is true that he finds *a single one* which would seem to be able to clarify the nature of social classes. Situated between 'mass societies' and 'uni- and multi-functional' groupings, the latter constitute for him 'supra-functional' groupings. Unfortunately, beyond the fact that this criterion tells us nothing about the social and historical function of classes, it is not even specific, for they share it with 'ethnic groupings and national minorities'. (*La vocation actuelle de la sociologie*, p. 298.)

14 Ibid., p. 275.

15 Ibid., pp. 272–3.

16 Ibid., p. 293.

17 P. Sorokin, 'Qu'est-ce qu'une classe sociale', *Cahiers internationaux de sociologie. II*, 2, 1947, p. 78. After having given this definition, Sorokin comments, one by one, on the eight points enumerated. We may relish particularly his commentary on point three: 'The interpretation of these different connections is "natural" and "normal" for each class. Usually a certain poverty accompanies manual work (skilled or unskilled) at the same time as a relative privation of privileges (*de jure* and *de facto*); a certain degree of wealth and a privileged status (*de jure* and *de facto*) sometimes go cheek by jowl with creative intellectual work' (ibid., p. 79).

If 'normal' is a statement of fact for Sorokin, it is singularly naïve to believe that 'creative' intellectuals enjoy a certain degree of wealth and privileged status (*de jure* and *de facto*). History teaches rather the contrary. On the other hand, if 'normal' is a desideratum, it is no less curious to learn 'that a certain poverty' is 'normal' for manual labour.

18 G. Gurvitch, *La vocation actuelle de la sociologie*, p. 345.

19 It is clear that here we are simply comparing the two theories without meaning to assert that Sorokin has had an influence on Gurvitch.

20 We are affixing this limit to our hypothesis simply because we have never studied antiquity sufficiently well to know if, in ancient societies, the situation, from this point of view, was analogous or different. (On the concept of world-view see E. M. Mendelson, 'World-View' in *International Encyclopaedia of the Social Sciences*, vol. 17, Macmillan & Free Press, New York, 1968. [Ed. Note])

21 It is obvious that there are also transitional phenomena between the classes which are reflected on the ideological plane. For example, see Lenin's well-known analyses of the

worker aristocracy and its relations with a reformist ideology. But just as a worker aristocracy is not a class, reformism, however important it might be as an ideological phenomenon, is not a *world-view*. There is indeed a reformist politics and sociology, but there is no reformist ethic, aesthetic or epistemology.

22 *La logique ou l'art de penser*, part III, chap. 19.

23 On the subject of Molière's comedies, see P. Bénichou, *Morales du grand siècle*, Gallimard, Paris, 1948.

24 The maximum of potential consciousness that Weber envisages is only for the individual consciousness.

25 Quesnay, founder of Physiocracy, was personal physician to Louis XV who printed the *Tableau économique* with his own hand. Quesnay began to occupy himself with economics at the age of sixty-two.

26 Charles Gide and Charles Rist, *Histoire des doctrines économiques*, Paris, 1909 (and several revised editions). With a certain amazement, Gide simply notes the attitude of Professor Henri Denis who declares 'that he is close to sharing Mirabeau's admiration'. The fact is that H. Denis read Marx in full. (Eng. trans., *A History of Economic Doctrines from the time of the Physiocrats to the Present Day*, Harrap, London, several editions from 1915–61. [Ed. Note])

27 On K. Kautsky, in English, see, *Terrorism and Communism*, Allen & Unwin, London, 1920; *The Economic Doctrines of Karl Marx*, A. & C. Black, London, 1925; *The Labour Revolution*, Allen & Unwin, London, 1925; *The Dictatorship of the Proletariat*, University of Michigan Press, Ann Arbor, 1964. On R. Hilferding, see, 'Bohm-Bawerk's Criticism of Marx', in E. von Bohm-Bawerk's *Karl Marx and the Close of his System*, A. M. Kelley, New York, 1949. (Ed. Note)

28 See J. Schumpeter, *Two Essays*, Meridian Books, New York, 1955, which contains a bibliography of his works. (Ed. Note)

CHAPTER IV

1 Lukács once defined form 'as the shortest way to the top'.

However, the two meanings that the word 'form' has in this section must be distinguished: the first, a *coherent* and *adequate* expression of a world-view, as opposed to eclecticisms; the second, a means of expression which is or is not adequate to the *content* that it expresses.

2 The example was partly suggested to us by Professor Théophile Spoerri.

3 The efforts of Dilthey and Jaspers seem altogether inadequate to us.

4 It is this common basis which explains, for example, the possibility of their reunion in the work of one and the same man, Montaigne, who yet never disavowed himself.

5 On this subject, see, L. Goldmann, 'Matérialisme dialectique et histoire de la philosophie', *Revue philosophique de France et de l'étranger*, 1948, nos 4–6; and L. Goldmann, 'Matérialisme dialectique et histoire de la littérature', *Revue de métaphysique et morale*, 1950, nos 7–9; reprinted in *Recherches dialectiques*, Gallimard, Paris, 1958.

APPENDIX

1 For a detailed study of Pascal and Racine, see our *Le dieu caché: Étude sur la vision tragique dans les Pensées de Pascal et dans le théâtre de Racine*, Gallimard, Paris, 1956.

2 It is true that one text which is ascribed to the year 1655, the celebrated *Entretien de Pascal avec Monsieur de Saci*, by Fontaine, could bring this chronology under question. But since this text appeared only after the death of Pascal, it might very well have been reviewed by him after 1657 or even have been drafted by Fontaine after a reading of the *Pensées*.

3 While we agree completely with Charlier and Orcibal about the relation between *Athalie* and the English Revolution, we interpret the relation differently.

SELECTED BIBLIOGRAPHY

The principal works of Lucien Goldmann, with the dates of their first appearance

LA COMMUNAUTÉ HUMAINE ET L'UNIVERS CHEZ KANT (Presses Universitaires de France, Paris, 1952)

SCIENCES HUMAINES ET PHILOSOPHIE (Presses Universitaires de France, Paris, 1952)

LE DIEU CACHÉ (ÉTUDE DE LA VISION TRAGIQUE DANS LES PENSÉES DE PASCAL ET DANS LE THÉÂTRE DE RACINE) (Gallimard, Paris, 1956)

RACINE (L'Arche, Paris, 1956)

CORRESPONDANCE DE MARTIN DE BARCOS, ABBÉ DE SAINT-CYRAN (Presses Universitaires de France, Paris, 1956)

RECHERCHES DIALECTIQUES (Gallimard, Paris, 1958)

POUR UNE SOCIOLOGIE DU ROMAN (Gallimard, Paris, 1964)

THE AUTHOR

Lucien Goldmann was born in Bucharest in 1913. After legal studies at the University of Bucharest and a year's philosophy in Vienna, he went to Paris in 1934 and obtained French degrees in law, political science and literature. After this, he worked for two years with Jean Piaget in Geneva. He joined the French Centre National de la Recherche Scientifique and, in 1956, took his doctorate at the Sorbonne. From 1958 onwards he was Directeur d'Études in the VIth section of the École Pratique des Hautes Études in Paris, teaching the sociology of literature and of philosophy. In 1961 he became Director of the Centre de Recherches de Sociologie de la Littérature at the Sociological Institute of the Free University in Brussels.

CAPE EDITIONS